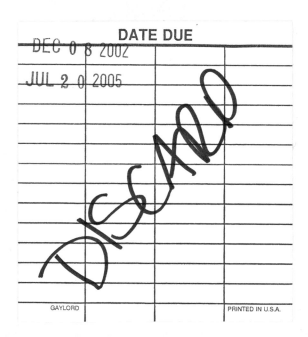

basic microwaving

microwave cooking library™

by barbara methven

microwave cooking library™

This is no ordinary recipe book. It's like a cooking school in your home, ready to answer questions on the spot. Step-by-step photographs show you how to prepare food for microwaving, what to do during cooking, how to tell when the food is done. A new photo technique shows you how foods look during microwaving.

The foods selected for this book are basic in several ways. All microwave well and demonstrate the advantages of microwaving. They are popular foods you prepare frequently, so the book will be useful in day-to-day cooking. Each food illustrates a principle or technique of microwaving which you can apply to similar recipes you find in magazines or other cookbooks.

All foods are cooked at either High or 50% (Medium). These settings are available on most ovens. They simplify the choice of settings while you become familiar with the reasons why different foods require different power levels.

Microwaving is easy as well as fast. The skills you develop with this book will help you make full and confident use of your microwave oven.

Barbara Methven

Barbara Methven

CREDITS:
Design & Production: Cy DeCosse Creative Department, Inc.
Consultant: Joanne Crocker
Home Economists: Jill Crum, Carol Grones, Sylvia Ogren, Maria Rolandelli, Sara Jean Thoms, Judy Tills
Photographers: Michael Jensen, Ken Greer, Jack Mithun, Warren Reynolds
Production Coordinators: Bernice Maehren, Dan Marchetti, Nancy McDonough
Color Separations: Weston Engraving Co., Inc.
Printing: R. R. Donnelley & Sons Company

Contents

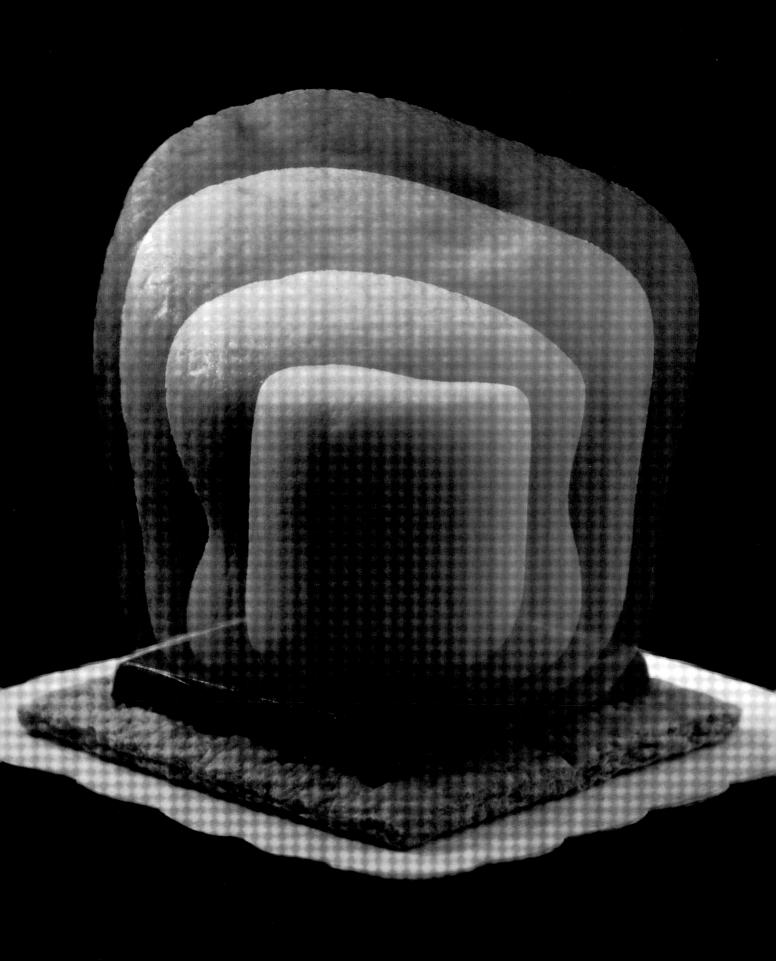

Multiple Exposure of S'mores through oven door at four second intervals demonstrates microwave speed.

Microwaving: What you Should Know before You Start

A wide variety of microwave ovens is available today to make almost all food preparation faster and easier. The directions in this book have been tested in all major brands of ovens, so you can use them with confidence in your oven.

All Ovens Do Not Cook Alike

Like conventional ranges, microwave ovens differ in their rate and evenness of cooking. House power differs from one part of the country to another. If you live in a small farming community, your appliance may cook faster than the same model in a large city. Voltage fluctuates and is lower during periods of peak consumption. An appliance will cook slower on extremely hot or cold days when more electricity is being used.

You Control the Cooking

A microwave oven is a cooking appliance. It may be faster and easier to use than a conventional appliance, but it still needs a cook to control it. Personal preferences differ. Food which is undercooked for one person may be overcooked for another.

To allow for differences in equipment, house power and personal tastes, both microwave and conventional recipes provide a time span during which food may be done, and a test by which you may determine doneness. Unless you have a fast oven and live in a high voltage area, the minimum time suggested in these directions will probably be too short. However, checking food at the minimum time will allow you to judge how much more time is needed.

The amount of attention (stirring, turning, etc.) suggested in our directions is based on the minimum needed for satisfactory results. No matter what type of oven you have, the more attention you give the food, the better the results will be. If you feel that food is not cooking evenly, you can usually correct this by stirring or turning more often, or by allowing a longer standing time.

Look While You Cook

Don't be afraid to watch your food through the oven door. The diffused light inside a microwave oven is due to the finely perforated metal screen imbedded in the door. This screen prevents the escape of microwave energy, while it allows you to look as you cook.

If food is ready to boil over, or is overcooking in one area, you can stop cooking immediately by opening the oven door or by pushing the stop button. This has the same effect as removing a pan from the range but it also stops microwave energy immediately. The oven cannot operate while the door is open.

Microwave Ovens are Safe

Microwave ovens are built for safety. They must be thoroughly tested to meet the standards of several regulating agencies.

Since a microwave oven is a miniature broadcasting system, the Federal Communications Commission makes sure that it does not broadcast on the wrong frequency.

Underwriters Laboratory assures that the oven is electrically safe when properly grounded and operated.

The Department of Health, Education and Welfare must approve the design of the oven, especially the door's safety interlock system.

Government regulations are strict and allow a wide margin for safety. In addition, the government requires that all oven manufacturers publish the following precautions. They assure that the oven, which is safe when you buy it, will remain safe while you use it.

Precautions to Avoid Possible Exposure to Excessive Microwave Energy

Do not attempt to operate the oven with the door open since open door operation can result in harmful exposure to microwave energy. It is important not to defeat or tamper with the safety interlocks.

Do not place any object between the oven front face and the door or allow soil or cleaner residue to accumulate on sealing surfaces.

Do not operate the oven if it is damaged. It is particularly important that the oven door close properly and that there is no damage to the (1) door (bent), (2) hinges and latches (broken or loosened), (3) door seals and sealing surfaces.

The oven should not be adjusted or repaired by anyone except properly qualified service personnel.

What are Microwaves?

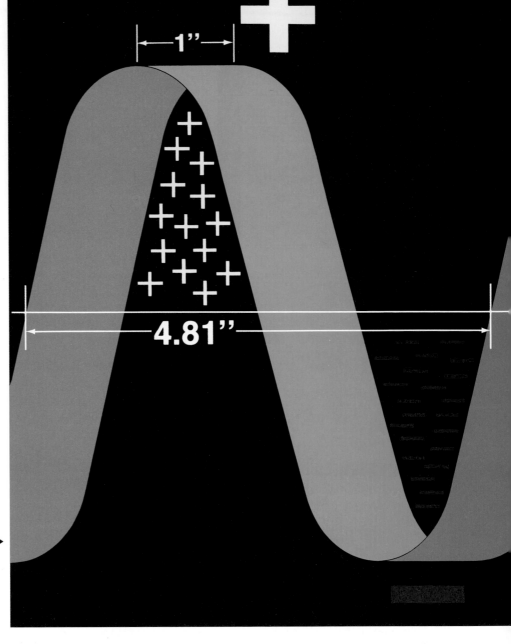

Microwaves are high frequency electromagnetic waves, like ordinary daylight and radio waves. Microwaves used in ovens are very short, less than 5 inches long, while radio waves vary in length from 3 feet to many miles.

Radio waves are in the air around us all the time. Radio energy can be broadcast from great distances, even from the moon, and is converted to sound in your radio. The microwave "broadcasting system" is contained within the oven, where the energy is converted to heat in food.

The microwave is an energy ▶ field which alternates in positive and negative directions, and acts like a magnet on the positive and negative particles in food molecules.

How Microwaves are Broadcast into the Oven

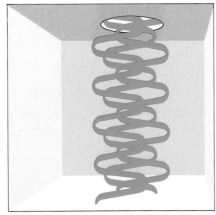

Energy enters the oven cavity through an opening in the metal case, usually at the top. Hot spots occur if it is not distributed in the oven or the food.

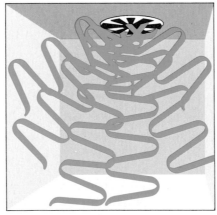

A Stirrer, similar to a fan blade, deflects microwaves to different parts of the oven so all do not follow the same path. Some ovens move food through the energy field on a turntable.

Microwaves cannot penetrate metal. They are reflected off the oven walls at right angles. There must be food in the oven to absorb the energy.

How Microwaves Cause Heat by Friction

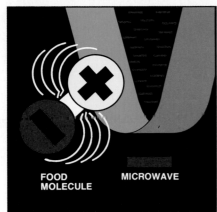

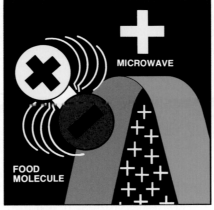

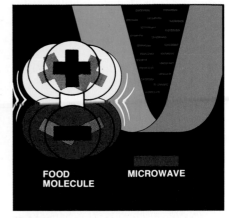

Opposites attract. Plus particles in food molecules are attracted to the negative or minus direction of the microwave.

Positive direction of the microwave attracts minus particles. Microwaves reverse direction 2,450,000,000 times a second.

Friction between molecules vibrating almost 2½ billion times a second produces heat in food.

How Microwaves Cook Food

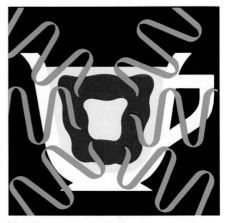

Microwaves penetrate food from all directions to a depth of ¾ to 1½-in. They cause no chemical change in the food.

Vibration of food molecules causes heat in the areas of penetration. These areas begin to cook.

Heat spreads through conduction to other parts of the food, as it does in conventional cooking.

How Microwaves Affect Water, Fat & Sugar Molecules

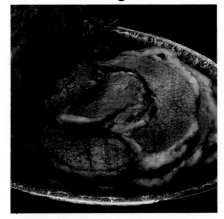

Water is driven to the surface of food during microwaving. This moisture evaporates but surface does not become crisp.

Fat is drawn to the surface, where it browns on long-term foods. Center of roast is cooked by heat conduction.

Sugar attracts microwave energy. Surface temperature of roll equalizes with air. Center becomes very hot and burns.

Food Characteristics & Microwaving

These food characteristics affect all cooking, but microwave speed makes the differences more pronounced. Water, fat and sugar attract microwave energy, so foods containing them cook faster. When several foods are cooked at once, microwave-attractive foods may draw energy away from foods which contain less water, fat or sugar and alter their cooking time.

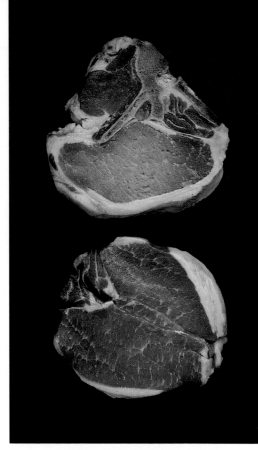

Size. Small pieces cook faster than large ones in both microwave and conventional cooking. Since microwaves penetrate food ¾ to 1½ inches, uniform pieces under 2 inches in diameter cook from all sides.

Shape. Thin parts of uneven foods cook faster than thick parts. Uniformly thick foods cook evenly. Place thin parts toward the center of the dish where they receive less microwave energy.

Quantity. Small amounts cook faster than large ones. Microwaving time is always directly related to the amount of food and increases with the quantity. When doubling a recipe, increase time by about ½ and check for doneness.

Amount of bone. Bone conducts heat. When bone is on side of meat, that side cooks first. Boneless cuts cook less rapidly but more evenly.

Quality. Fresh vegetables microwave best. Test by cutting. Moisture should appear on surface rapidly. If it takes more than a minute, add more water.

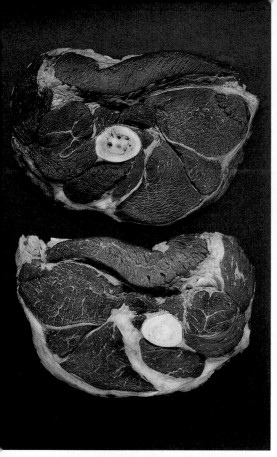

Fat distribution. Evenly distributed fat tenderizes and helps cook meat evenly. Large fatty areas attract energy away from meat and slow cooking.

Density. Dense, heavy foods like brownies take longer to microwave than porous, airy ones like cake. A food changes in density with the way it is prepared. Solid beef is denser than ground; baked potatoes hold their heat longer than mashed.

Starting temperature. Room temperature foods cook faster than refrigerated or frozen ones. Room temperature varies with the season. Cooking times may be longer on a cold winter day.

Moisture content. Add a minimum of water to fresh or frozen vegetables. Extra water slows cooking. Foods with low moisture do not microwave well.

Precooking. Fresh vegetables need time to tenderize. Frozen vegetables have been blanched and may take less time, even though they are frozen. Some brands of frozen vegetables are almost fully cooked and need only defrosting and heating.

Microwave Techniques:
Comparison with Conventional

Start with what you already know. Most techniques used in microwaving are the same ones used when cooking conventionally. There may be differences in application but they are easy to understand once you compare cooking methods.

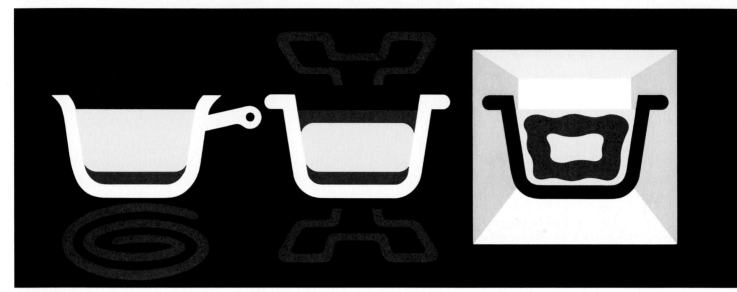

Range Top. The surface burner on your range becomes hot and transfers heat to the bottom of the pan. This in turn heats the bottom of the food. To cook evenly and prevent burning, you must turn food over or stir cooked portions from the bottom to the top.

Conventional Oven. Heating elements in a conventional oven heat the air. This hot air heats the surfaces of food from all directions. Slowly the heat transfers from the surface to the center of the food. Since air in the oven is hot and dry, the surface of food becomes dry.

Microwave Oven. Microwaves penetrate food from all directions to a depth of ¾ to 1½ inches. Heating takes place beneath the surface; there is no heat in the oven itself. The center of food over 2 inches thick cooks by heat transference, as it does conventionally.

Covering food holds in steam to tenderize it and speed cooking in both microwave and conventional methods.

Stirring equalizes temperature in food and shortens cooking time. Since microwaves cook from all directions, you should stir from outside to center of dish. Ovens vary in amount of stirring needed, but all cook more evenly with occasional stirring.

Turning Food over is done in both range top and microwave cooking to help it heat evenly. When microwaving, turn over large, dense foods such as whole vegetables or roasts, which might cook more near the top of the oven.

Arranging food in oven when cooking several items is done in both types of cooking. Use ring pattern for microwaving.

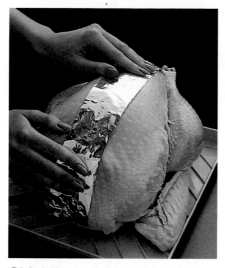

Shielding protects sensitive areas from overcooking in both the conventional and microwave oven.

Rearranging food in the dish or on the oven shelf is done conventionally, but is used more often when microwaving. Corners or sides of dish receive more energy. Some places in oven may be warmer than others. Rearranging helps foods cook evenly.

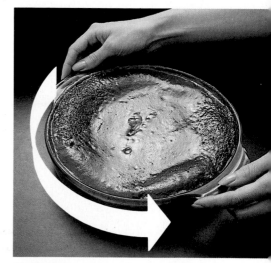

Arranging uneven foods with thinner areas toward the center of dish prevents overcooking. Thicker parts, which take longer to cook conventionally, receive more microwave energy and will be done at the same time as thinner or more delicate areas.

Rotating, or turning in the oven, is used with foods which cannot be stirred, rearranged or turned over.

Microwave Techniques:
Covering

Covering serves much the same purpose in microwaving as it does in conventional cooking. While there is little evaporation during microwaving, a cover holds in steam to tenderize food, keep it moist and shorten cooking time.

In general, foods which you cover conventionally should be covered during microwaving. Remove covers carefully; steam can cause burns.

Loose casserole cover allows some steam to escape. In most cases this makes little difference. A sheet of wax paper may be placed between casserole and lid to make it tighter.

Tight cover fits snugly over rim of casserole, leaving no gaps for steam to escape. Use this type of cover when steaming vegetables which do not require added moisture.

Tight cover of plastic wrap can be used with dishes which do not have covers.

Vent plastic wrap by rolling back one edge to form a narrow slot. A tight cover of plastic wrap may split during microwaving unless you provide an opening for excess steam to escape.

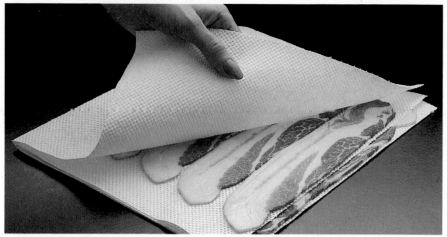

Dry paper towel allows steam to escape while it prevents spatters and absorbs excess moisture. Use to cover bacon, or foods which are cooked uncovered but tend to spatter.

Wax paper forms a loose cover similar to "partial covering" in conventional cooking. Use it to hold in heat, speed cooking and prevent spatters with foods which do not need steam to tenderize.

Cooking bag holds in steam to tenderize meat. Before microwaving, remove any foil from bag and discard metal twist tie. Tie loosely with string or strip of plastic cut from end of bag; leave small space for steam to escape. Place bag in cooking dish.

Paper towels absorb moisture trapped between food and oven floor, and keep bread surfaces dry.

Damp towel steams scallops or fish fillets. To soften tortillas, heat 4 at a time between moist towels; 10 to 20 seconds at High.

Microwave Techniques:
Dish Shapes, Shielding, Standing

Using the right dish or casserole is important in microwaving. Both size and shape affect the way foods cook, the attention needed and microwaving time. Get to know your casserole sizes.

Depth of the container is as important as capacity. Both of these casseroles hold 1½ quarts of food, but the deeper one takes longer to microwave. A shallow casserole exposes more food surface to microwave energy.

Round shapes microwave more evenly than squares or rectangles. More energy penetrates corners, which may overcook.

◄ **Avoid** casseroles with sloping sides. Food is less deep in the areas which receive most energy and can overcook. A straight sided casserole keeps the depth of food uniform.

Ring shapes are excellent for foods which cannot be stirred during microwaving. Energy penetrates food from the center as well as the sides, top and bottom for faster, more even cooking.

14

Dramatic experiment demonstrates the affect of shielding. Wrap ice cube in foil and place in oven with a glass of water. Microwave until water boils.

Unwrap ice cube; it will still be ▶ frozen because microwave energy cannot penetrate metal. Note, water continues to boil.

Shield foods which attract mi- ▶ crowave energy with a sauce to keep them moist. When microwaving casseroles, bury pieces of meat in sauce or vegetables. Use small strips of foil on thin areas to prevent overcooking.

Reduce power level when microwaving dense foods, such as roasts, or delicate foods like custard. The lower power level protects foods from a high concentration of energy and helps them cook evenly.

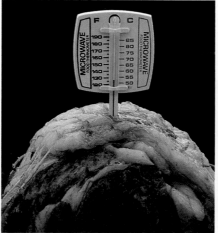

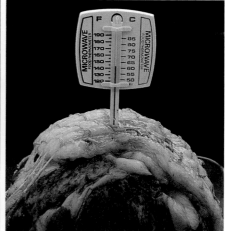

High foods may require shielding or turning over. Areas close to the top of the oven receive more energy.

Standing time allows microwaved foods to finish cooking by internal heat after they are removed from the oven. The internal temperature of this roast rose from 125° to 140° during 15 minutes standing. Roast is also easier to carve after standing.

Microwave Techniques:
Testing for Doneness

Start with what you already know. The appearance of some microwaved foods may be different from conventionally cooked, but many tests for doneness are the same. The final test is your own preference. Some people like food crisp; others prefer it very soft. Adjust cooking times to suit yourself.

The directions in this book tell you when to test for doneness and what to look for. Standing is part of the microwaving process. Wait until after standing time before taste-testing food. You can always microwave a little longer, but nothing can save food which is overcooked. Standing is especially important for foods which need time to tenderize or which toughen when overcooked.

Wooden pick inserted in center of cake comes out clean. Moist spots on surface will dry on standing. Do not insert pick in moist spot.

Cake pulls away from sides of pan when done. Top will not be brown, but cake will be higher and lighter than conventionally baked.

Knife inserted halfway between center and edge of custard comes out clean. Center appears soft but will set on standing.

Raw shellfish are gray and translucent. They turn pink and opaque when cooked. To avoid toughening, undercook slightly and let stand.

Fish flakes easily with fork. Center is slightly translucent but cooks on standing. Fish toughens and dries if overcooked.

Meat is done when fork tender. Less tender cuts split at fibers. Allow standing time to tenderize them.

Drumstick of chicken moves freely at joint and is soft when pinched. Last juices drained from cavity run clear yellow.

Most testing techniques are the same as the ones you learned for conventional cooking, but there are a few which are unique to microwaving.

When food is brought to a boil on an electric burner, it continues to cook after the burner is turned off. Manufacturers call this "coasting time" and advise you to use it to save energy. Few cooks do; they take the pan off the stove.

With microwaving, heat is inside the food. You can't stop cooking by removing food from the oven. Use the heat to finish cooking and save energy.

Feel the bottom when reheating a plate of food. It will be warm when food is hot enough to transfer heat to the dish.

Remove some foods from the oven while they still look partially cooked. This is the hardest thing to learn about microwaving, although standing time is also used conventionally to allow foods to settle.

Be patient and let the food stand. If it isn't done to your taste after standing, you can microwave a little longer, but there's no remedy for overcooking.

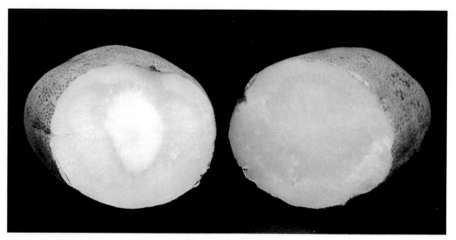

Potato is heated through after 5 minutes of microwaving, but when cut it reveals an uncooked center. After standing 5 minutes the center is completely cooked. Potatoes hold their heat up to 45 minutes when wrapped in foil.

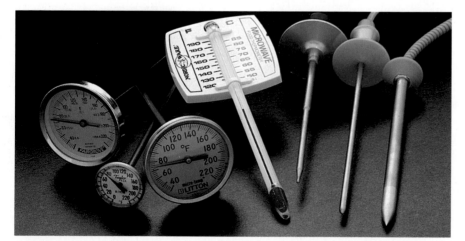

Probes and microwave thermometers register the internal temperature of meat. Insert them as you would a conventional meat thermometer. A probe shuts the oven off automatically when the meat reaches a pre-set internal temperature. It is not accurate for poultry because the fat becomes hot rapidly and a probe may turn the oven off before the meat is fully cooked.

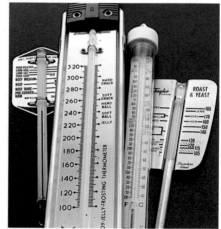

Do not use conventional meat or candy thermometers. They may be used to check temperatures outside the oven, but only microwave thermometers can be used during cooking.

Microwave Techniques:
Browning

People who have never used a microwave oven before are sometimes concerned about browning because they don't know what to expect. Once they become familiar with microwaving, many cooks feel that browning is unimportant.

The appearance of some foods may be slightly different from conventionally cooked, but microwaved foods look cooked, not raw.

Some foods do brown. Examples are roasts with a good fat covering, bacon, whole chickens and turkey breasts. These foods have a high fat content which comes to the surface quickly and browns.

With the exception of bacon, these browned foods will not be crisp. Chicken pieces take less time to microwave than a whole chicken and do not have time to brown.

Browning Utensils

These utensils, designed specifically for microwaving, sear and brown foods the way a conventional skillet does. They should never be used with a conventional range.

Browning utensils have a special coating on the bottom which absorbs microwave energy and reaches a temperature of 500° to 600°. The sides and handles of the utensils stay cool. Feet or ridges raise the bottom to protect counters, but hot browning utensils should not be placed on plastic mats or table tops.

Browning grill well catches fat and juices so steaks and chops don't steam. Paper towels or wax paper should never be used to reduce spatters. They could catch fire, as they would on a range top, because of high heat generated by dish.

Browning dish sides and cover prevent spatters. When meat is browned, sauces can be added for continued cooking in the same dish.

How To Use Browning Utensils

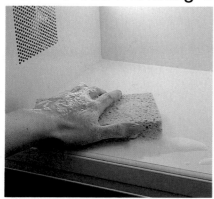

Be sure oven is clean. Grease will bake onto oven floor or shelf when dish is preheated.

Preheat dish as manufacturer directs. Preheat only ½ to ⅔ of time before adding butter.

Do not use non-stick sprays or coatings with browning utensils; they scorch.

Microwave Techniques:
Browning Agents

Some foods do not brown during microwaving. While many cooks find them unnecessary, browning agents can be used to give microwaved foods an appearance similar to conventionally cooked. Many browning agents flavor foods, too.

Plain microwaved hamburger► loses its gray color on standing. For browner color and added flavor, sprinkle meat with onion soup mix before microwaving.

Plain microwaved chicken has a light golden color. Piece on the right was brushed with melted butter and sprinkled with paprika before microwaving.

Microwaved cakes do not brown. Top or frost them as you would a conventionally baked cake.

How to Use Browning Agents

Choose a browning agent appropriate for your food from the chart. Browning agents can be savory, sweet or unflavored. Some liquids are applied full strength, but most are diluted with equal parts of water or butter. Dry agents are sprinkled on before or during microwaving.

Brush on liquid browning agents before microwaving. Soy sauce gives meat an oriental flavor. Bouquet sauce colors with little flavoring.

Browning Agent & Coating Chart

Agent	Foods	Comments
Soy or Teriyaki Sauce	Hamburgers, Beef, Lamb, Pork, Poultry	Brush on meat; rub into poultry
Barbecue Sauce	Hamburgers, Beef, Lamb, Pork, Poultry	Brush on or pour over
Melted Butter and Paprika	Poultry	Brush on butter; sprinkle with paprika
Brown Bouquet Sauce and Melted Butter	Hamburgers, Beef, Lamb, Pork, Poultry	Brush on meat; rub into poultry
Worcestershire or Steak Sauce and Water	Hamburgers, Beef, Lamb, Pork	Brush on
Onion Soup or Gravy Mix, Bouillon Granules	Hamburgers, Beef, Lamb	Sprinkle on before microwaving
Taco Seasoning Mix	Hamburgers, Savory Quick Breads	Sprinkle on before microwaving
Bread Crumbs, Bread Crumbs and Parmesan Cheese, Crushed Corn or Potato Chips	Casseroles	Sprinkle on after final stirring
Crushed French Fried Onion Rings, or Crumbled Bacon and Shredded Cheese	Savory Quick Breads, Casseroles	Sprinkle on before microwaving or after final stirring
Brown Sugar, Chopped Nuts, or mixture of both	Cakes, Sweet Quick Breads	Sprinkle on halfway through or after microwaving
Cinnamon-Sugar or Coconut	Sweet Quick Breads	Sprinkle on before microwaving
Powdered Sugar	Cakes	Sprinkle on after microwaving
Jelly, Preserves or Glazes	Ham, Poultry	Glaze ham after microwaving; poultry after ½ cooking time

Dry chicken thoroughly. Rub liquid agents into skin before microwaving. Dilute bouquet sauce with butter.

Glaze ham or poultry with jelly, preserves or glazes for sheen and flavor. See chart for methods.

Sprinkle on dry toppings as directed. Casseroles which require stirring should be topped after last stirring.

Microwave Techniques:
Combine Microwave with Conventional Cooking

Many foods are prepared most efficiently when you do part of the cooking by microwave and part conventionally. Use microwaving for its speed, easy clean up and unique jobs which cannot be done conventionally.

Microwave fillings and sauces for crepes you prepare with a crepe maker or skillet.

Prepare and fill crepes in advance. Refrigerate until serving time, then microwave until hot.

Toast bread conventionally. Prepare sandwiches and microwave to heat fillings and melt cheese.

Brown meats in a pyroceram® casserole on the conventional range. Microwave as directed in this book, but reduce time by ¼ to ⅓.

Warm syrup for pancakes in serving pitcher or uncapped bottle. Reheat leftover pancakes, too.

Soften brown sugar. Place apple slice in bag. Close tightly with string or plastic strip. Microwave ¼ minute at High or until lumps soften.

Shell nuts which are difficult to remove whole. Microwave 8 ounces of nuts in 1 cup water 4 to 5 minutes at High.

Plump raisins. Sprinkle 1 or 2 teaspoons of water over fruit. Cover tightly. Microwave ½ to 1 minute at High.

◄ **Blanch** almonds. Microwave 1 cup water until boiling. Add nuts. Microwave ½ minute at High. Drain and skin.

Make instant mashed potatoes right in the measuring cup. Place water, butter and salt in cup. Microwave until boiling. Add milk to correct measure. Stir in flakes.

Peel tomatoes or peaches easily. Put enough water to cover food in a casserole or measuring cup. Microwave until boiling. Drop in food for a few seconds. Peel strips off quickly.

Melt chocolate in its paper wrapper or a plastic cup you've already used to measure milk or shortening. It won't scorch and you'll save dishwashing. Use 50% power.

Melt butter for blender hollandaise, basting sauces and frostings for conventional cakes.

Microwave sauces while you cook pasta conventionally. Reheat pasta without flavor loss.

Soften gelatin. Measure water into a bowl or 4-cup measure. Microwave until boiling, stir in gelatin and cold water.

Microwave chicken or ribs until almost done. Finish on barbecue grill for charcoal flavor. Interior will be fully cooked without overbrowning.

Grill extra hamburgers while the coals are hot. Undercook slightly and freeze. Defrost and finish by microwaving.

Soften cream cheese directly from the refrigerator. For dips and spreads, it can be softened right in the serving dish.

◄ **Get** more juice from lemons. Microwave 20 to 35 seconds at High before cutting and squeezing.

Microwave Utensils

Some materials are transparent to microwaves. Energy passes through them as light passes through a window, and heats the food inside.

Metal reflects microwaves. The metal does not get hot, but reflected energy can overheat materials next to it.

Microwave utensils can become hot, but the heat comes from food, not microwave energy. Heat sensitive materials can be used for warming but not cooking foods.

Paper products can be used for heating and serving foods, or as light covers to absorb moisture and spatters during cooking.

Plastic, such as foam dishes and dishwasher safe containers can be used for heating, but melt or distort at cooking temperatures.

Plastic Films and cooking bags hold in steam to tenderize foods and speed cooking.

Packages, such as wax-coated freezer wrap and plastic-coated boxes, can be placed in the oven for defrosting.

Microwave Plastics are designed especially for microwave cooking. Use them as the manufacturer recommends.

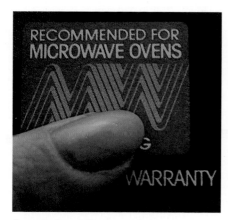

Look for labels reading "Microwave Oven Safe" or "Suitable for Microwave". Check the warranty for heating and cooking information.

Oven glass and glass ceramic (pyroceram) are among the most versatile microwave utensils. Make sure they have no metal trim or screws in lids or handles.

Stoneware, which is safe for use at low and medium conventional temperatures, is excellent for microwave cooking and serving.

Pottery, porcelain and china, which cannot be used for conventional cooking, can be used for microwaving.

Metal Rims and signatures on dishes will darken and may cause the dish to crack.

Foil Trays under ¾-in. deep can be used, although heating will occur only on exposed top surface. Deeper pans take too long to heat. Keep foil at least 1-in. away from oven walls.

Metal Pans reflect energy and slow cooking so much that all microwave advantage is lost.

Foil Lined packages, used for some dairy products, dry foods and take-home foods, shield the food from microwave energy. Do not attempt to defrost or reheat foods in these packages.

Microwave Utensils continued

You don't need a cupboardful of new equipment to use with your microwave oven. Many utensils you already have are suitable for microwaving, including some things you never before thought of as cooking utensils.

Some utensils are designed especially for microwaving. Browning dishes and grills are discussed on page 19.

Many of the new microwave utensils do double duty and can be used in a conventional oven, too. Before using any plastic utensil, read the manufacturer's instructions. While plastics are transparent to microwave energy, some of them are sensitive to heat from food and will melt or distort when used to cook foods which reach high temperatures.

Microwave Utensils You May Already Have

Oven glass custard and measuring cups, pie and baking dishes, casseroles and mixing bowls are all suitable for microwaving. You can measure, mix and cook in one utensil.

Pyroceram®casseroles and skillets can be used with microwave and conventional ovens as well as on the range. They're good for combination cooking.

Special Microwave Utensils

Test dish if you are not sure it is microwave oven-safe. Place it in oven. Measure ½ to 1 cup water in glass cup. Place on or beside dish. Microwave 1 to 2 minutes at High. If dish remains cool it is suitable for microwaving.

Deep cake pans allow for the greater volume of microwaved cakes. Fluted molds provide a traditional bundt shape.

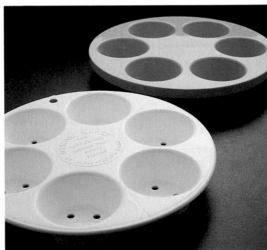

Muffin makers arrange food in a ring. Some offer ventilation on the bottom to reduce moisture.

Pottery and stoneware serving dishes, cups and plates can be used to cook and serve. Food stays hotter when it's cooked in the serving dish, and you have less clean-up.

Porcelain ramekins, soufflé, quiche and au gratin dishes are both microwave and conventional oven-safe.

Paper and plastic products you use for casual meals, food storage and clean up are useful microwave cooking utensils.

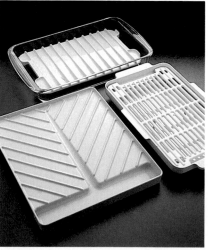

Baking sheets provide a broad surface for large items and foods cooked in quantity.

Roasting racks are available as a molded in one piece utensil, or as an insert for a glass utility dish. They elevate meat so it doesn't steam in fat and juices.

Ovenable paper can be used for heating food in any type of oven. It's freezerproof, too, so you can make your own freezer-to-microwave-to-table entreés.

Microwave Techniques:
Defrosting

Defrosting frozen food is one of the benefits of a microwave oven. Most ovens have a Defrost setting, but the power level assigned to it may vary from 70% to 30%. In this book, defrosting times are given for 50% and 30% because one of these settings is found on most ovens, although neither may correspond to the Defrost setting.

The final quality of the food you defrost depends on two factors. The first is good freezer management. Food should be properly packaged and not stored too long. The second is attention to the food while microwave-defrosting.

Lower power levels reduce the amount of attention needed during defrosting. At lower levels, the oven cycles on and off. During the "off" periods, heat has time to equalize. The photograph below shows what happens when 1-lb. of hamburger is defrosted without attention at various power levels.

Microwaves are attracted to water, not ice. As soon as some ice crystals melt, they draw energy away from frozen areas. This heated water melts channels through the block of frozen food.

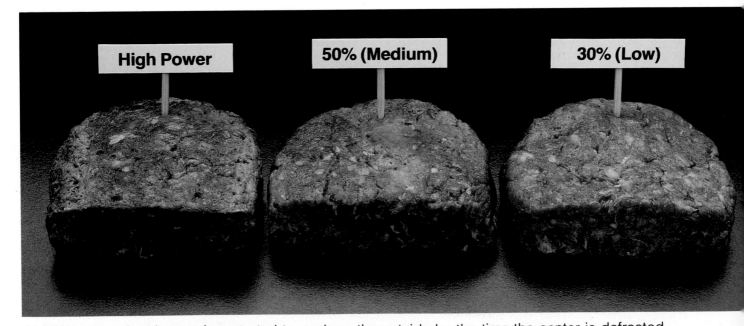

At High power hamburger has started to cook on the outside by the time the center is defrosted. At 50% power fewer areas have begun to cook. At 30% cooked areas are minimal, even without attention. Breaking up and removing defrosted parts improves defrosting at any power.

Flex pouches and packages which cannot be broken up or stirred. This distributes heat.

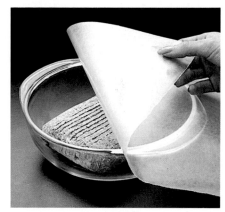

Cover meat with wax paper. It will hold warmth around food as it begins to defrost.

Defrosted areas begin to cook and change color before frozen parts are thawed unless the block is broken up and redistributed.

Tips to Speed Defrosting

Remove styrofoam tray as soon as possible when defrosting meat. It insulates bottom of meat like an ice chest. The paper liner used to absorb meat juices will draw energy from meat unless removed.

Pour off liquid from poultry frozen in plastic bag. It absorbs energy and slows defrosting.

Microwave Techniques:
Reheating

How to Reheat Meats

Most foods reheat in the microwave oven without loss of quality or texture. They taste freshly cooked, not warmed-over. Main dishes reheat especially well; some even improve in flavor if they are made in advance. Care must be taken to avoid additional cooking; rare meat should never be heated beyond its original doneness temperature, or it will cook to medium or well done.

Never reheat meats at High power. Refrigerated main dishes should be reheated at 50% power. Individual plates of food heat best at a lower power setting.

Thin slices of meat reheat more evenly than thick slices.

How to Reheat Main Dishes

Always cover main dishes. If they have been refrigerated, reheat at High.

Stir main dishes and casseroles, if possible, to distribute heat.

Rotate main dishes which cannot be stirred and microwave at 50% power (Medium).

How to Reheat Plates of Food

Arrange plate with thick or dense foods to outside and delicate foods to center of plate.

Spread out main dishes to a shallow, even layer for quick, uniform heating.

Cover plate with wax paper or plastic wrap to hold in heat and moisture.

Arrange thick portions of food to outside of dish as you do when cooking.

Add sauce or gravy to dry meats to provide moisture.

Cover with wax paper. When reheating dry meat without sauce, place paper towel under wax paper.

How to Reheat Vegetables

Saucy vegetables, such as scalloped potatoes, reheat well. Stir if possible, or rotate dish.

Moist or starchy vegetables reheat with a fresh taste when well wrapped.

Fibrous vegetables, such as artichokes, asparagus or broccoli lose texture when reheated.

How to Reheat Breads

How to Reheat Desserts

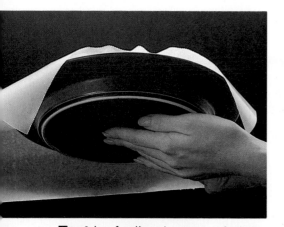

Test by feeling bottom of plate. When food is hot enough to transfer heat to plate, it's ready.

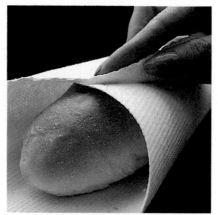

Wrap in paper towel to absorb moisture. Bread toughens if over-heated. One roll takes only 8 to 12 seconds.

Reheat carefully. Sugary fillings get very hot, although pastry or cake may remain cool.

Microwave Techniques:
Menu Planning

Like any other meal, a microwave menu should provide sound nutrition and attractive contrasts of color, flavor and texture. It's easy to microwave an entire meal when your plan takes advantage of standing and holding time and the fact that microwaves reheat foods without loss of flavor or quality. The sample menus show you how.

Early in the day, prepare foods like puddings, which need to be chilled, or cakes which are served at room temperature.

Advance cooking of foods which reheat easily simplifies meal preparation and improves the flavor of foods like hot German potato salad, spaghetti sauce and many casseroles.

Meatloaf Dinner

Meatloaf, page 60

Twice-Baked Potatoes, page 109

Broccoli Spears, page 113

Tossed Salad

French Apple Pie, page 135

Serves 4 to 6

Early in the day:
Microwave pie. Wash, dry and refrigerate salad ingredients.

At least 45 to 60 minutes before serving time:
Microwave potatoes and assemble meatloaf. If convenient, this may be done earlier.

35 minutes before serving time:
Microwave meatloaf. Prepare broccoli and stuff the potatoes while meatloaf is in the oven.

Microwave broccoli while meatloaf is standing. It will hold up to 20 minutes after standing. Reheat the potatoes. While they are heating, toss the salad.

If you wish to serve the pie warm, reheat it while clearing the table for dessert.

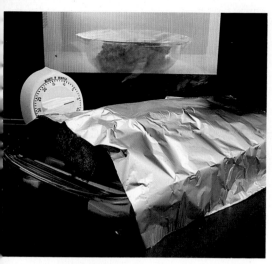

Long standing time required for large, dense items like roasts, can be used to microwave another food.

Holding time of foods which retain heat well allows you to keep them hot while you microwave the rest of the meal.

Last minute preparation should be reserved for foods which cool quickly, like peas; heat in seconds, like rolls; or do not reheat well, like nachos.

Fiesta Supper

Chili, page 54

Rice, page 122

Nachos, page 43

Tossed salad of endive, orange wedges and onion rings

Peanut Scotch Bars, page 139

Serves 4 to 6

Early in the day:
Microwave Peanut Scotch Bars. Prepare and refrigerate salad ingredients.

At least 1 hour before serving:
Microwave chili. It may be prepared as early as the day before and refrigerated when it is cool.

At least 20 minutes before serving:
Microwave rice and prepare nachos for heating. If chili has been cooked in advance, allow time to reheat it. Rice will hold 20 minutes, covered.

Just before serving:
Heat nachos and toss salad. A second plate of nachos can be heated while the first is being served with the meal.

33

Menu Planning continued

When you are planning a meal so that every food will be hot and ready to serve at the same time, three factors must be considered in addition to actual microwaving time.

Standing time is a part of the cooking process; it is used to complete cooking and tenderize the food. Where standing time is necessary, it is included in the microwaving directions.

Holding time is the length of time a properly wrapped or covered food will retain its heat after standing is completed. For example, one potato takes 3 to 5 minutes microwaving time and 5 to 10 minutes standing time. Wrapped tightly in foil or plastic, it will keep hot an additional 45 minutes. You can start your potato any time from approximately 10 to 60 minutes before serving time. That gives you plenty of flexibility in planning and microwaving a meal.

Reheating time is the time needed to bring a precooked food back to serving temperature. When you are planning a meal it should be added to the total time required to complete the meal.

Holding Time Techniques & Factors Which Affect Holding Time

Depending on their size and density, foods can be kept warm for some time after the standing time is completed. Cook food in the serving dish to lengthen the time it will remain hot. If the food requires standing time to complete cooking, holding time is calculated from the end of standing time.

Fish, casseroles and vegetables should be tightly covered. Wrap large, whole vegetables in plastic or foil. Cover meats loosely to avoid a steamed taste. Meats which are cooked in a plastic bag or tightly covered dish should be left covered.

Foods cool off faster when there are many surfaces exposed to air. While standing times are approximately the same, a whole cauliflower remains hot far longer than cauliflowerets.

Wrapping foods extends holding time. After standing time, corn in the husk holds 10 to 12 minutes. Corn in plastic wrap stays hot 40 minutes.

Holding Time Chart

Long Holding Time 20 to 45 minutes	Medium holding time 10 to 20 minutes	Short holding time 3 to 10 minutes
Ham	Chicken	Chops
Roasts weighing over 4 lbs.	Ham slice	Fish fillets
Turkey	Meatloaf	Hamburgers
Beans, baked	Roasts weighing 2 to 4 lbs.	Carrots, sliced
Cauliflower, whole	Most casseroles	Corn, whole kernel
Corn on cob, plastic wrapped	Broccoli	Beans, green or wax
Potatoes, baked	Carrots, whole	Mushrooms
Potatoes, scalloped	Cauliflowerets	Peas
Sweet potatoes, whole	Corn on cob, in husk	Bread
Sweet potato casserole	Potatoes, mashed	Rolls, sweet
Winter squash casserole	Rice	Cake
	Squash, acorn	Pie, slice
	Pie, whole	

Reheating Chart

Three factors are important in reheating: the starting temperature, quantity of food, and whether or not it can be stirred. A plate of food set aside for a latecomer will probably be at room temperature, but most foods should be refrigerated if they are to be held more than 2 hours. If you are reheating a refrigerated plate of food, add ½ to ⅓ more time and check frequently after 3 minutes. If reheating a casserole, vegetable or dessert and the food is still at room temperature, reduce the time slightly and check while stirring or rotating.

Large quantities of refrigerated leftovers which cannot be stirred, such as 4 to 6 servings of lasagne, should be reheated at 50% power. Double the time, check and rotate the food frequently during the second half of reheating time.

Amount	Starting Temp.	Power Level	Time	Comments
Plate of Food 1 serving meat, 2 servings vegetables	Room	High	1½-2 min.	Arrange meaty portions and bulky vegetables to outside of plate. Cover with wax paper.
Meat (chicken pieces, chops, hamburgers, meatloaf slices)				
1 serving	Refrigerated	High	¾-1½ min.	Cover with wax paper.
2 servings	Refrigerated	High	1½-3 min.	
Meat Slices (beef, ham, pork, turkey)				
1 or more servings	Refrigerated	50%	¾-1 min. per serving	Shield with gravy, or cover with paper towel. Cover with wax paper. Check after 30 seconds per serving; rotate more than 1 serving.
Casseroles and Main Dishes				
1 serving	Refrigerated	High	2-4 min.	Cover with wax paper. Stir or rotate after ½ the time. When large amounts can't be stirred, microwave at 50% power.
2 servings	Refrigerated	High	4-6 min.	
4-6 servings	Refrigerated	High	6-8 min.	
Vegetables				
1 serving (½ cup)	Refrigerated	High	¾-1½ min.	Cover with wax paper.
2 servings (1 cup)	Refrigerated	High	1½-2½ min.	
Rice				
1 serving (¾ cup)	Refrigerated	High	¾-1½ min.	Cover with wax paper.
2 servings (1½ cups)	Refrigerated	High	1½-2½ min.	
4 servings (3 cups)	Refrigerated	High	1¾-3 min.	
Rolls, Dinner or Breakfast				
1	Room	High	8-12 sec.	Wrap single rolls in paper towel or napkin. For several rolls, line plate or bread basket with paper towel or napkin and cover rolls with second towel or napkin.
2	Room	High	11-15 sec.	
4	Room	High	18-22 sec.	
Pancakes				
4 (4 to 6" diameter)	Refrigerated	High	¾-1¾ min.	Place on paper towel lined plate.

Microwave Techniques:
Recipe Conversion

Many of your favorite recipes can be converted for microwaving with few changes other than a shortened cooking time. Select foods which microwave well. Use this book as a guide, since the foods and techniques included here are basic to microwave cooking.

What to Look for in a Conventional Recipe

Similar cooking techniques. Conventional recipes which call for steaming, moist cooking, covering and stirring will be good microwave recipes, too.

Moist foods. Naturally moist foods, such as chicken pieces, seafood, vegetables and fruits microwave well. Check the microwaving directions for these foods, since they will need less added moisture than called for in your conventional recipe.

Saucy foods. Most casseroles and main dishes cooked in a sauce adapt easily to microwaving and will have the same flavor and texture as they do when conventionally cooked.

Rich foods. Candies, bar cookies and rich moist coffee cakes microwave well because of their high fat or sugar content.

How to Convert a Conventional Recipe to Microwave

Follow guidelines below to convert recipes for microwaving. Check food often. Mark changes on the recipe for future use.

Find a similar microwave recipe and start with the same amount of the main solid ingredient.

Reduce liquid to about ¾. You may add more during microwaving if necessary.

Use slightly less seasoning, especially with strong flavors. You can correct to taste later.

Compare the amount of added fat. Fat attracts energy and slows cooking of other foods.

Follow the microwave recipe for dish size, covering, microwaving techniques and timing.

Reduce conventional time to ¼ or ⅓ if you do not have a microwave recipe as a guide.

Some Conventional Recipes Should Not be Converted

Fried foods such as crisp fried chicken, hash browns or French fried potatoes cannot be microwaved. Never try to deep fat fry in a microwave oven.

Crusty foods such as popovers, pancakes, pizza and 2-crust pies either do not form a crust or become soggy on the bottom.

Yeast breads cannot be converted from conventional baking. Use a specially formulated microwave recipe.

Uncooked pasta, rice or dried beans need time to absorb moisture. Other ingredients combined with them may overcook before they are tender.

These examples illustrate the way in which recipes can be converted. The first was selected because it is simmered in sauce, using similar cooking techniques, the second by comparison with a microwave recipe. Changes were based on the conversion guidelines.

Chicken Cacciatore

1 2½ to 3-lb. broiler-fryer, cut up
¼ cup olive oil
1 large onion, sliced
½ medium green pepper, chopped

2 cloves garlic, minced
1 can (16-oz.) Italian tomatoes
1 can (8-oz.) tomato sauce
¼ cup dry red or white wine
1 teaspoon salt
1 teaspoon crumbled oregano
¼ teaspoon pepper
1 or 2 bay leaves

In large skillet, brown chicken in olive oil. Remove chicken from skillet. Saute onion, pepper and garlic until tender. Add remaining ingredients. Return chicken to skillet. Simmer, covered, 45 minutes. Turn chicken in sauce. Cook uncovered 20 minutes more, or until chicken is tender and sauce is thickened.

What to watch for:

Chicken cooked in sauce.

Omit or reduce to 1 to 2 tablespoons (for flavor only).

Use 1 clove.

Drain and reserve liquid.

Use 1 for milder flavor.

Use large casserole or baking dish.

Omit these steps. No need to sear chicken.

Optional; if using olive oil for flavor, microwave onion, pepper and garlic in oil 3 to 4 minutes.

Arrange chicken in sauce with meatiest parts to outside of dish.

Microwave 10 minutes at High. Turn chicken in sauce. Cover. Microwave 9½ to 12½ minutes more, adding some of reserved tomato liquid if sauce is too thick.

Chili Con Carne

1 medium onion, chopped
½ green pepper, chopped
1 lb. ground beef
1 can (8-oz.) tomato sauce
1 cup water or beef broth
1 teaspoon salt
1 to 2 tablespoons chili powder
1 can kidney beans

Brown onion, green pepper and meat together. Add tomato sauce, water and seasonings. Simmer 15 minutes. Taste for seasoning. Add beans and simmer 2 hours.

Compare with recipe on page 54.

Same amount of meat. No tomatoes. Uses water and undrained kidney beans for liquid. Reduce water to ½ cup.

Start with 1 tablespoon.

Follow method on pages 54 and 55. Add more water or broth if needed for desired consistency. Correct seasonings after microwaving.

Beverages

Start microwaving by boiling water. Simple experiments with liquids demonstrate several microwave techniques. You can heat beverages in their serving cups, even paper or plastic hot drink cups. If you like brewed tea, you can boil water in the teapot, unless it has metal trim or a wicker-wrapped handle over a metal base. Heating liquids will illustrate the effects of quantity, starting temperature and food characteristics.

Instant beverages are prepared by heating water right in the cup. It takes less than 2 minutes to boil water for a single serving.

How to Microwave Liquids

Arrange cups in a ring with space between them when heating more than two. Leave the center empty.

Boiling time depends on the amount of water heated and whether it came from the tap hot or cold.

Watch through the oven door when heating milk-based liquids. They boil over rapidly. As boiling starts, open the oven door.

Spiced Cider

⅓ cup brown sugar
⅓ cup water
2 teaspoons whole cloves
2 sticks cinnamon

1 teaspoon whole allspice
¼ teaspoon salt
2 qts. cider

Makes approx. 2 quarts

Combine sugar, water and seasonings in 4-cup measure. Microwave at High 4 to 6 minutes to form a light syrup. Combine with cider in 3-qt. casserole. Microwave 7 to 9 minutes, until heated. Strain before serving.

Irish Coffee

For each serving:
1 to 2 teaspoons light brown sugar

⅔ cup strong black coffee
1 jigger (1½-oz.) Irish whiskey
Whipped cream

Dissolve sugar in coffee in an Irish coffee cup or coffee mug. Microwave at High 1 to 2 minutes, until very hot. Add whiskey and top with whipped cream.

Appetizers

These two dips call for different forms of cheese. Notice that cream cheese is softened at High power, then heated gently at 50% power. Cheese food, which attracts energy, is melted at 50% power. When thinned with other ingredients, it is heated briefly at High.

Zippy Dip

4 oz. cream cheese
¼ cup catsup
2 to 3 tablespoons chopped
    green onion
3 drops Tabasco

        Makes approx. 1 cup

Soften cream cheese in 1-qt. casserole at High 20 to 25 seconds. Pour catsup into 1-cup measure. Cover; microwave ½ to 1 minute until bubbly. Stir into cheese with onion and Tabasco. Microwave at 50% (Medium) 1½ to 2½ minutes, until hot.

Cheese Dip

1 pkg. (1-lb.) processed
    cheese spread, cut in
    1½-in. cubes
¼ cup beer
1 clove garlic, crushed
1 tablespoon chopped
    pimiento, optional
1 tablespoon snipped
    parsley, optional

        Makes approx. 2 cups

Cocktail Wieners

1 pkg. (1-lb.) wieners
1½ cups barbecue sauce
2 tablespoons brown sugar
⅛ to ¼ teaspoon dry mustard
½ teaspoon ginger

        Makes approx. 1 quart

Photo directions opposite.

How to Microwave Cheese Dip

Place cheese spread cubes in 2-qt. casserole. Microwave at 50% power 3 to 6 minutes or until melted, stirring once.

Beat in beer and garlic with wire whip until smooth. Microwave at High until heated, about 1 minute. Garnish with pimiento and parsley.

How to Microwave Cocktail Wieners

Cut wieners into ¾-in. pieces. Set aside. Combine sauce, sugar and seasonings in a 1½-qt. casserole or serving bowl. Cover. Microwave at High 1½ to 2½ minutes, until hot.

Stir in wieners; cover. Microwave 4 to 6 minutes, stirring once. When hot, serve with cocktail picks.

Bacon Stix

Bacon Stix can be assembled in advance and stay crisp several hours after microwaving.

10 thin bread sticks, any flavor
 5 slices bacon, halved lengthwise
½ cup grated Parmesan cheese

Makes 10 stix

Photo directions opposite.

Shrimp in Garlic Butter

¼ cup butter or margarine
½ teaspoon garlic powder
 2 teaspoons parsley flakes
 1 pkg. (12-oz.) frozen, peeled, deveined, quick-cooking shrimp

Makes 1½ to 2 cups shrimp

Photo directions below.

How to Microwave Shrimp in Garlic Butter

How to Microwave Bacon Stix

Place butter in custard cup. Microwave at High 30 to 45 seconds until melted. Stir in garlic powder and parsley flakes. Separate shrimp; place in 9 or 10-in. diameter dish.

Pour butter mixture evenly over shrimp. Cover tightly. Microwave 5 to 8 minutes, until shrimp are opaque, stirring every 2 minutes. Let stand, covered, 1 to 1½ minutes.

Dredge one side of bacon strip in cheese; roll it against bread stick diagonally.

42

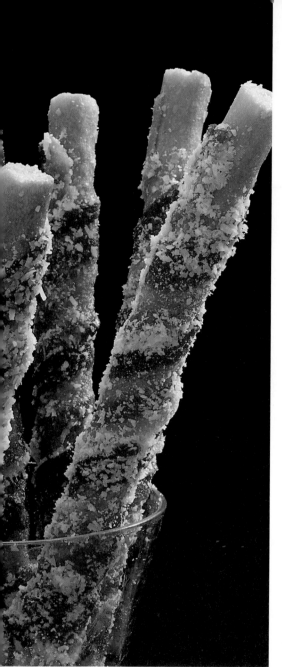

Nachos

16 large tortilla chips
4 oz. shredded Monterey Jack cheese
2 tablespoons shredded cheddar cheese, optional

Makes 16 Nachos

Photo directions below.

Variation:

Zippy Nachos: Place a small slice of jalapeno pepper or stuffed olive on each chip before sprinkling with cheese.

How to Microwave Nachos

Place sticks on baking sheet, dish or paper plate lined with paper towels. Microwave at High 4½ to 6 minutes. Roll again in cheese.

Place a sheet of wax paper on a 10-in. glass or paper plate. Cover with tortilla chips.

Sprinkle with cheese. Microwave at 50% power (Medium) 1½ to 2½ minutes, until cheese melts, rotating once or twice.

Hot Munchies

Each of these recipes makes enough canapé spread for 24 melba toast rounds or dry, crisp crackers. If the recipe calls for cream cheese, soften it at High 15 to 30 seconds before adding remaining ingredients.

Hawaiian Chicken

3 slices cooked bacon, crumbled
1 5-oz. can chicken meat
¼ cup lightly drained, crushed pineapple
¼ cup walnut pieces, chopped
¼ teaspoon salt
   Dash pepper

Far-East Tuna

3¼ oz. tuna, drained
   3 tablespoons mayonnaise
   3 tablespoons finely chopped pecans
   3 tablespoons drained, crushed pineapple
   ⅛ teaspoon curry powder

Midwest Bacon & Cheese

6 slices cooked bacon, crumbled
½ cup shredded cheddar cheese
3 tablespoons mayonnaise
1 teaspoon parsley flakes
1 teaspoon caraway or poppy seeds, optional

Seashore Crab

3 oz. cream cheese, softened
5 oz. crab meat
2 teaspoons Worcestershire sauce
½ teaspoon lemon juice
2 tablespoons chopped green onion

Classic Ham 'n Cheese

4½ oz. deviled ham spread
   2 tablespoons finely chopped onion
   ¼ cup shredded cheddar cheese
      Sliced stuffed olives, as garnish

How to Microwave Hot Munchies

Combine ingredients in a small bowl. Spread ½ the mixture on 12 melba or other crackers. Arrange on paper plate.

Microwave at High 30 to 60 seconds, until heated, rotating plate ¼ turn after 20 seconds. Repeat with remaining mixture and crackers.

Stuffed Mushrooms

These hot and tasty mouthfuls are the star attraction of any collection of appetizers. Each recipe stuffs 8 ounces of fresh mushrooms.

Spinach Filled

6 oz. frozen spinach soufflé
¼ cup shredded cheddar cheese
¼ cup seasoned bread crumbs
¼ teaspoon thyme
¼ teaspoon salt

Remove soufflé from foil, divide in half with sharp knife. Return half to freezer. In small bowl, defrost at 50% for 2 to 5 minutes, or until soft. Mix in other ingredients.

Cheese & Walnut

Chopped mushroom stems
3 oz. bleu cheese, crumbled
½ cup chopped walnuts
¼ cup seasoned bread crumbs

Microwave stems. Stir in cheese. Add walnuts and bread crumbs, reserving 2 to 3 tablespoons of each. Stuff mushrooms, garnish with reserved nuts and crumbs.

Ham & Cream Cheese

Chopped mushroom stems
3 oz. cream cheese, softened 15 to 30 seconds on High
½ cup finely chopped ham
¼ cup finely chopped almonds

Classic

Chopped mushroom stems
1 small onion, finely chopped
2 tablespoons butter or margarine
1 tablespoon parsley
⅓ cup seasoned bread crumbs
¼ teaspoon salt
⅛ teaspoon garlic powder

Smoked Cheese & Salami

Chopped mushroom stems
2 tablespoons onions, finely chopped
⅓ cup processed smoked cheese spread
¼ cup seasoned bread crumbs
¼ cup finely chopped salami

How to Microwave Stuffed Mushrooms

Wash 8-oz. fresh mushrooms. Remove and chop stems. Place stems in small bowl with onion or butter, if included in recipe. Cover with plastic wrap.

Microwave at High 1½ to 2½ minutes, until tender. Stir in remaining ingredients. Mound in mushroom caps.

Arrange caps on paper towel lined plate with larger caps to outside. Microwave 1½ to 3 minutes, until heated, rotating plate once or twice.

Meats & Main Dishes

Meats microwave in ⅓ to ½ the time it takes to cook them conventionally. They stay juicy because they are not exposed to hot, dry air. For the same reason, their surface will not become dry and crisp.

The flavor of microwaved meats may be slightly different, due to retention of natural juices and lack of a seared surface. If you wish to sear meats, use a browning dish or grill.

Defrosting meat is an important advantage of a microwave oven. Microwave defrosting is not only faster, it can help retain meat quality. Frozen meat begins to lose its juices as soon as it is thawed. For best results it should be cooked immediately. With a microwave oven you can time defrosting so the meat will be at its best when you are ready to cook it.

Main dishes are another microwaving specialty. They're fast and flavorful. If you use precooked meats, they won't have a leftover taste, and leftover main dishes reheat easily.

Selecting & Storing Meat for Microwaving

Meat is an important part of the menu and a major item in the food budget. Select and store meat carefully for the best flavor and freshness. Place it in the coolest part of the refrigerator as soon as you bring it home, and use within the recommended time.

Well-marbled beef microwaves best. This is true of less tender cuts as well as tender steaks and roasts. Beef should have fine streaks of smooth, white fat distributed throughout the lean. During microwaving, the fat melts and tenderizes the meat.

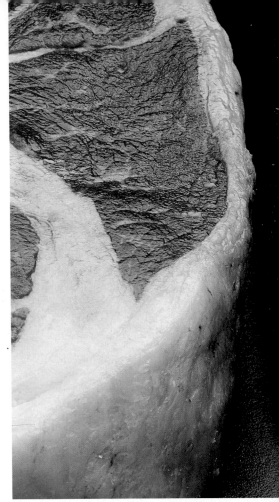

Compare the amount of meat juices lost in microwaving with conventionally cooked results. For this demonstration, uniform portions of lean ground beef were placed in cooking bags to prevent evaporation, and cooked to an internal temperature of 180°.

Chuck roast is well-marbled and usually costs less than leaner cuts of less tender beef. It's a good microwave choice.

Use ground beef within 24 hours. It spoils more rapidly than solid meat because more surface is exposed to bacteria. Store other meat in the original package up to 2 or 3 days. If you do not plan to use it within that time, place meat in a lemon juice, wine or vinegar marinade as soon as you bring it home. A marinade tenderizes, flavors and preserves meat about 5 days.

Select pork chops which are free of excessive moisture and have firm white fat. Avoid wet looking pork with crumbly, milky colored fat. Use pork within 2 days.

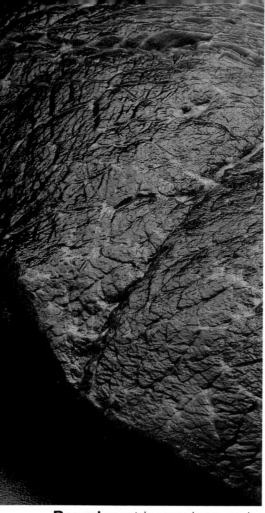

Round roast is very lean and has little marbling. It will be more chewy than chuck roast when microwaved.

Cut a boneless chuck roast into 1-inch cubes for beef stew. Supermarket stewing meat is usually cut from the leaner round, and piece size may be irregular. Small pieces microwave best and you can be sure they are uniform when you cut them yourself.

Plain Ground Beef   Lean Ground Beef   Extra Lean Ground Beef

Fat covering helps tenderize lean roasts. Some markets sell roasts with a fat layer secured by string or mesh. Strips of bacon, held with string or wooden picks, add flavor.

Ground beef is sold in several grades. Since microwaving extracts fat, regular ground beef will shrink and make main dishes fatty. Most of our directions call for lean ground chuck. Extra-lean ground round is an excellent choice for dieters.

Freezing and Defrosting Meat for Microwaving

Meat should be wrapped as air tight as possible before freezing. Air draws moisture from meat and produces ice crystals which cause dry, white areas called "freezer burn". For best quality, freeze meat quickly by placing it next to the wall of the freezer.

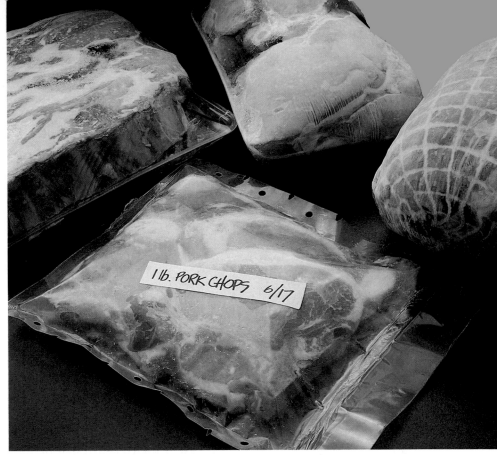

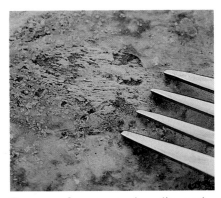

Freezer burn can be discarded easily during microwave-defrosting. Simply pick off the hard, dry areas with a fork.

Freeze meat in original packages for storing 1 to 2 weeks. For longer storage, rewrap meat tightly in wax-coated freezer paper, or package in heat-sealable bags. Press out as much air as possible before sealing. Label with contents, weight and date.

Package bulk ground beef in ▶ convenient, ready-to-use forms.

1. Pre-make hamburger patties. Stack with plastic wrap or doubled wax paper between layers. Wrap tightly in freezer paper. To use, remove as many patties as needed and reseal package. Use this method for chops and steaks.

2. Divide beef into 1 or 1½-lb. packages. Most recipes call for these amounts.

3. Use shallow plastic freezer boxes for freezing and defrosting; follow manufacturer's directions. Deep freezer containers are difficult to defrost.

4. Pre-cooked ground beef keeps longer than raw meat. Microwave meat, with chopped onion or green pepper if you like, until it loses its pink color. Cool quickly and freeze in recipe-sized amounts for casseroles and main dishes.

How to Defrost Ground Beef

Ground beef is easiest to defrost when it is frozen in recipe-size amounts. During the final defrosting period, check meat occasionally. Remove or scrape off softened parts, especially when defrosting amounts over 1 pound.

50% Power (Medium)
3¾-4¾ minutes per lb.

30% Power (Low)
5-7 minutes per lb.

Place paper or plastic wrapped package or freezer box in oven. Defrost for ⅓ of time. Turn over. Defrost for ⅓ of time.

Twist fork in meat to break up. Remove soft pieces. Defrost remaining time. Break up amounts over 1-lb. part way through.

Let stand 5 minutes (1-lb.) to 10 minutes (over 1-lb.). Meat will still contain ice crystals, but will be pliable.

How to Defrost Cubed Meat   50% (Medium) 3-4 min. per lb.; 30% (Low) 7½-9 min. per lb.

Place package in oven. Defrost for ½ the total time. Unwrap and separate cubes.

Spread cubes out in casserole or baking dish. Remove any defrosted pieces.

Defrost for second ½ of time. Let stand 5 minutes, or until they can be pierced with fork.

How to Defrost Chops 50% (Medium) 3-4 min. per lb.; 30% (Low) 5½-7 min. per lb.

Place package in oven. Defrost for ½ the total time.

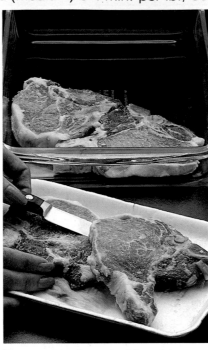

Separate chops with table knife. Arrange in baking dish with least defrosted parts to outside of the dish.

Defrost for remaining time. Let stand 5 minutes, or until chops can be pierced with a fork.

How to Defrost Roasts over 2-inches Thick 50% (Medium) 5-6½ min. per lb. 30% (Low) 9½-11½ min. per lb.

Place package in oven. Defrost for ¼ the total time.

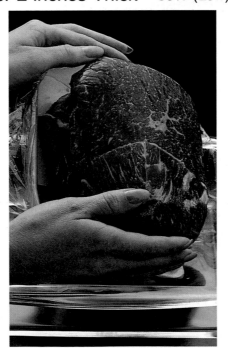

Unwrap roast. Remove plastic tray and paper liner, which slow defrosting.

Shield any warm areas with foil. Turn roast over into baking dish.

How to Defrost Steaks & Flat Roasts

50% (Medium) 3½-4½ min. per lb.
30% (Low) 7-9 min. per lb.

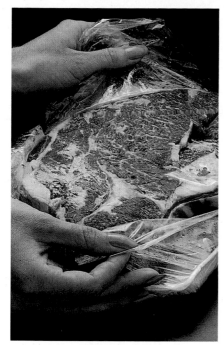

Place package in oven. Defrost for ½ the time. Remove wrapping, plastic tray and paper liner.

Shield any warm areas with foil. Turn meat over into baking dish. Defrost for remaining time.

Let stand 5 minutes. Meat is defrosted when it can be pierced to center with a fork.

Defrost second ¼ of time, or until surface yields to pressure. Let stand 10 minutes.

Defrost for third ¼ of time. Turn roast over; shield warm areas. Defrost remaining time.

Let stand 20 to 30 minutes, or until a skewer can be inserted to the center of roast.

Ground Beef

Chili

- 1 lb. ground beef, regular or lean
- 1 medium onion, sliced
- 1 medium green pepper, chopped
- 1 clove garlic, minced
- 1 can (16-oz.) stewed tomatoes*
- 1 can (15½-oz.) kidney beans, drained
- 1 can (8-oz.) tomato sauce
- 1½ to 2 teaspoons chili powder
- 1 teaspoon salt
- ¼ teaspoon oregano

Makes about 2 quarts

*Drain for very thick chili

Photo directions below.

Chili and spaghetti sauce do not require standing time to complete cooking, but they benefit from advance preparation. Make them early in the day, or even the day before, to blend and enhance flavors. They reheat easily for serving. If you plan to refrigerate them, you can use regular ground beef. The fat will solidify and be easy to remove. Select lean ground beef if you wish to serve them immediately.

How to Microwave Chili or Spaghetti Sauce

Crumble ground beef into a 2-qt. casserole, or place in a casserole and break up with a wooden spoon.

Microwave at High power 3½ to 4½ minutes until meat is almost cooked.

Pour off fat. (If you are making this dish in advance, and plan to refrigerate it, omit this step.)

Spaghetti Meat Sauce

1 lb. ground beef, regular or lean
1 small onion, finely chopped
1 stalk celery with leaves, finely chopped
1 small carrot, finely chopped
1 clove garlic, minced
1 can (16-oz.) Italian plum tomatoes, undrained and coarsely chopped, or 1 can (16-oz.) stewed tomatoes
1 can (6-oz.) tomato paste
¾ cup dry red wine or beef broth
1½ teaspoons basil or oregano
1 teaspoon salt
1 teaspoon parsley flakes
¼ teaspoon pepper
1 small bay leaf

Makes about 2 quarts

Photo directions opposite.

Cook the pasta conventionally while you microwave the sauce; they'll be ready at the same time. To serve North Italian style, return drained pasta to its hot pot. Pour sauce over the pasta and toss together. Pasta prepared in this way can be reheated by microwave without losing its "al dente" texture.

Break up meat into smaller pieces. Stir in raw vegetables. Microwave 4 to 5 minutes until vegetables are tender.

Stir in remaining ingredients. Cover. Microwave 5 minutes at High power. Remove cover and stir.

Microwave uncovered at 50% of power (Medium) for 20 to 25 minutes, stirring at least once.

Meatballs

Meatballs can be prepared and served several ways. Make them small or large. They can be fully cooked without added moisture and served with Swedish Cream Gravy. They can be partially cooked, then finished in a sauce and served over pasta or rice. This mixture makes 12 large (2-in.) meatballs or about 20 small (1½-in.) balls. Directions are given for Swedish and Saucy Meatballs. Fix them your favorite way or try both for variety.

Meatball Mixture

1 lb. lean ground beef	1 teaspoon salt
1 egg	1 teaspoon basil or dill weed*
¼ cup chopped onion	½ teaspoon garlic powder
¼ cup fine dry bread crumbs	⅛ teaspoon pepper

Photo directions below.

*For Swedish Meatballs follow gravy directions on page 103.

High Power

Large Meatballs	7-9 min.
Small Meatballs	8-10 min.
Saucy Meatballs	Add 2-5 min. to total cooking time

How to Microwave Meatballs

Moisten palms of hands to shape large meatballs. Use a heaping tablespoon to form small ones easily.

Arrange large meatballs in a ring in a 10-in. dish or pie plate. Place small meatballs in an 8×8 or 12×7-in. dish.

Meatball Variations

Microwave at High 4 to 5 minutes. Rotate large meatballs or rearrange small ones, bringing balls from the outside of dish to the center.

Swedish Meatballs. Microwave remaining time. Set meatballs aside. They will brown on standing. For gravy, follow directions on page 103, using cream for ½ the liquid.

Saucy Meatballs. Pour off fat while rearranging. Add 1 can (8-oz.) tomato sauce or 1 can (10¾-oz.) mushroom soup, diluted with ¼ to ½ cup milk. Microwave remaining time.

Hamburgers

Hamburgers microwave easily because of their uniform consistency and even fat distribution. When they are served in buns with condiments, a browning agent is not needed for appearance. Picture shows a hamburger without browning agent. The charts are for ½-in. thick hamburgers, weighing ¼-lb. apiece.

High Power

Medium-Rare

Patties	1st side Minutes	2nd side Minutes
2	1½	¾-1
4	2	1-2
6	3	3¼-3½

Medium-Well

Patties	1st side Minutes	2nd side Minutes
2	2	1½-2½
4	2½	2-3
6	3½	3¼-3½

How to Microwave Hamburgers on a Plate or Roasting Rack

Brush or sprinkle with browning agent, if desired. Soy sauce, onion soup mix, or steak sauce and water or butter add flavor.

Arrange hamburgers on a roasting rack in a baking dish or on a plate lined with paper towel. Rack drains off fat while paper absorbs it; this improves flavor and reduces calories. Cover with wax paper to prevent spatters. Microwave on first side.

58

Preheated Browning Dish or Griddle Method

Preheat browning dish or griddle as manufacturer directs. Glass cover on browning dish may be used to prevent spatters, but griddle should be used uncovered. Microwave first side. Turn hamburgers over and rearrange them if you are cooking more than four. Microwave second side. Standing time is not needed.

High Power

	Medium-Rare		Medium-Well	
Patties	1st side Minutes	2nd side Minutes	1st side Minutes	2nd side Minutes
2	1	¾-1¼	2	1-2
4	2	1-2	2½	2-3
6	2½	2¼-2¾	3	3-3½

Turn hamburgers over. If you are microwaving more than 4 patties, rearrange them at this time, so those in the center of the dish are moved to the outside. Microwave minimum of remaining time. Check for doneness. They will cook a little more on standing.

Let hamburgers stand, covered with wax paper, 1 to 2 minutes. Gray color will turn brown but surface will not be crusty.

59

Meatloaf

Meatloaves remain moister when microwaved than they do when baked conventionally, so this mixture contains no milk or water. If you want to adapt a favorite meatloaf for microwaving, reduce the liquid by about half.

Microwave meatloaves by time, rotating them during cooking, and test for doneness with a probe or thermometer. (145° to 155°). They should be firm to the touch on top.

Basic Meatloaf

Mix together thoroughly:

  2 eggs, lightly beaten
1½ lbs. lean ground beef
  ¼ cup fine bread crumbs
  1 small onion, chopped
  2 tablespoons
     Worcestershire sauce
  1 teaspoon seasoned salt
  ½ teaspoon dry mustard
  ¼ teaspoon pepper

Spread over top, if desired:

  2 tablespoons catsup, steak, barbecue or chili sauce

Serves 4 to 5

High Power

Round	12-18 min.
Ring-shaped	8-13 min.
Loaf	13-18 min.
6 Individual	10-13 min.

How to Microwave Meatloaf

Spread mixture evenly in dish. For ring-shaped meatloaves, form mixture into large balls and pack into dish. This reduces cracking.

How to Select Meatloaf Shapes

Microwaved meatloaves come in many shapes. Which one you select depends on your oven's cooking pattern and on your own taste. A different shape can vary the presentation of a popular item on the menu.

Loaf shape is traditional. It tested successfully in all ovens at ▶ High power when rotated after half the cooking time. If your oven overcooks the corners, reduce power level to 50% (Medium) and microwave for twice the time.

Round meatloaves may be pie or ring-shaped. Use a 10-in. pie plate. The ring shape works well in most ovens. The ring is deeper than a pie-shaped meatloaf but energy penetrates from the center for even cooking. If you don't have a ring-shaped dish, place a 6-oz. custard cup in center of a 2-qt. casserole.

Individual meatloaves. Pack mixture into six 6-oz. glass custard cups. Arrange in ring in oven. Rotate after ½ the cooking time.

Top with sauce. For fewer moist spots and browner surface, leave uncovered.

Microwave, rotating dish after half the cooking time.

Let stand 5 to 10 minutes. It will complete cooking and become firm. Use this time to microwave vegetables for dinner.

Less Tender Beef

Swiss Steak

Four factors help tenderize this less tender cut. Pounding and cooking in tomato sauce break down fibers. A lower power level allows meat to simmer slowly. Standing time is the most important; meat will not be tender without it.

2 lbs. beef round or chuck, cut in serving size pieces
¼ to ⅓ cup flour
1 envelope onion soup mix
1 can (8-oz.) tomato sauce
2 teaspoons parsley flakes
¼ cup water

Serves 4

How to Microwave Swiss Steak

Pound meat with edge of saucer or meat mallet to tenderize and flatten it to ¼ to ½-in. thickness.

Coat meat with flour by shaking in a paper bag or dredging on a sheet of wax paper.

Place meat in 2-qt. baking dish. Sprinkle with soup mix.

Combine remaining ingredients in a 2-cup measure. Pour over meat. Cover with vented plastic wrap.

Microwave at 50% power (Medium) 25 minutes. Rearrange meat. Re-cover. Microwave 25 to 35 minutes longer.

Meat should be fork tender. Let stand, tightly covered, 10 minutes to tenderize further.

Beef Stew

In this recipe, beer is used to tenderize but not flavor the meat. For a true Flemish Beer Stew, use a full can of beer rather than 1 cup.

To prepare Beef Bourguignonne substitute dry red wine for the beer. Omit the brown sugar and add a can of sliced mushrooms with the peas.

    3 tablespoons flour
1½ lbs. beef chuck, cut in
       ¾-in. cubes
1½ cups cubed potatoes
       (½-in. cubes)
    1 cup sliced carrots (¼-in.
       slices)
    2 medium onions, sliced
    1 cup beer
    1 can (8-oz.) tomato sauce
    1 clove garlic, crushed
    1 tablespoon beef bouillon
       granules
  ½ to 1 tablespoon brown
       sugar
1½ teaspoons Worcestershire
       sauce
    1 teaspoon salt
  ⅛ teaspoon pepper
    1 cup (½ of 10-oz. pkg.)
       frozen peas, optional

Serves 4 to 6

How to Microwave Beef Stew

Toss flour and beef together in a 3-qt. casserole until beef is coated. Add remaining ingredients except peas. Cover.

Microwave at 50% power (Medium) for 50 to 60 minutes, until beef is fork tender, stirring once to help distribute heat.

Stir in peas. Microwave 10 minutes more. Let stand, covered, 10 to 15 minutes to tenderize meat.

Pot Roast

Four factors help tenderize microwaved pot roasts. The long standing time is most important. The meat will not be tender without it. A lower power setting allows meat to cook gently and absorb flavors.

Smothered Pot Roast

2½ to 3 lb. eye of round roast
   1 can (10½-oz.) cream soup, undiluted (celery, potato, mushroom)
   1 envelope onion soup mix

50% Power (Medium)
25-30 minutes per pound

How to Microwave Smothered Pot Roast

Puncture meat with a fork on all sides. This allows flavoring and moisture to reach interior.

Spread about ⅓ of cream soup in bottom of cooking bag. Place roast on top of soup.

Sprinkle soup mix evenly over meat. Cover with remaining undiluted cream soup.

Gather end of bag together; tie loosely with plastic strip, leaving small space for steam to escape.

Microwave at 50% power (Medium) for ½ the total time. Turn roast over. Microwave remaining time.

Let roast stand in bag 20 to 30 minutes to complete tenderizing. Serve meat thinly sliced with its sauce.

Liquid provides moisture and a cooking bag holds in steam. Cut a strip of plastic from the top of the bag to use as a closure. Do not slash the bag to vent, as it will be turned over during cooking and juices may escape.

Old-Fashioned Pot Roast

2 to 3½ lb. boneless chuck roast

Sauce:

¼ cup tomato paste
½ cup water
1 tablespoon instant beef bouillon granules
½ teaspoon thyme
½ teaspoon salt
1 bay leaf

Vegetables:

4 medium carrots cut in 1-in. lengths (2 cups), halve thick carrots lengthwise before slicing
1 medium onion, cut in eighths
1 large potato, cut in ½-in. cubes (1½ cups)

TIP: Freeze remaining tomato paste in small glass jar. To use, defrost in microwave oven until surface softens and you can scrape off amount needed.

How to Microwave Old-Fashioned Pot Roast

Place roast in cooking bag. Combine sauce ingredients; pour over meat. Close bag as shown for Smothered Pot Roast.

Microwave at 50% power (Medium) for ½ the total time. Turn roast over. Open bag carefully; steam can burn.

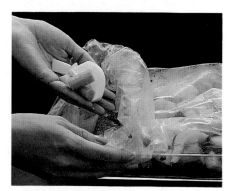

Add vegetables to bag and reseal. Microwave remaining time. Let stand in closed bag 20 to 25 minutes.

Pork Chops

Microwaved pork chops need to be encased in a crumb crust to hold in juices, or masked with a dense sauce to provide moisture.

You may use the methods photographed here with your favorite coating recipe or other flavors of condensed soup.

Crumb-Coated Pork Chops

4 pork chops, ½-in. thick
1 envelope prepared coating
  mix

Photo directions below.

Smothered Pork Chops

4 pork chops, ½-in. thick
1 can (10¾-oz.) mushroom
  soup

Photo directions opposite.

50% Power (Medium)
16½-18½ minutes per pound

How to Microwave Crumb-Coated Pork Chops

Shake pork chops with coating as directed on package, or toss with crumbs in paper bag.

Arrange chops in 8×8-in. dish with meaty portions to outside. Cover with wax paper. Cook at 50% power for ½ the time.

Rearrange chops so less cooked areas are to outside of dish. Discard wax paper. Microwave for second ½ of time.

How to Microwave Smothered Pork Chops

Arrange chops in 8×8-in. dish with meaty portions to outside. Spread undiluted mushroom soup over chops.

Cover with vented plastic wrap. Microwave at 50% power (Medium) for ½ the cooking time.

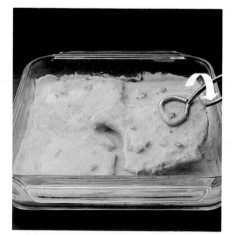

Turn over or rearrange chops. Replace plastic wrap. Microwave for remaining time.

Ribs

Ribs contain a lot of bone in proportion to meat, and can dry out and toughen if cooked too quickly. Microwave them briefly at High to get them started, then reduce the power to 50%.

Barbecued Ribs

2 lbs. pork ribs, cut in serving pieces
⅔ cup barbecue sauce
½ to 1 teaspoon liquid smoke, optional

Serves 2 to 4

2 Pounds Ribs

High Power   3 min.
50% Power   25-35 min.

How to Microwave Barbecued Ribs

Arrange ribs in single layer on a microwave baking sheet or 12×8-in. dish.

Combine sauce and liquid smoke in measuring cup. Brush ribs with ½ of sauce. Cover with wax paper. Microwave at High 3 minutes.

Reduce power to 50%. Microwave for 15 minutes. Turn ribs over and rearrange.

Brush with remaining sauce. Re-cover with wax paper.

Microwave 10 to 20 minutes, until meat is fork tender. Let stand, covered, 10 minutes.

Ham

Fully cooked hams need only be heated to serving temperature. The shorter microwaving time for canned hams is due to their flat shape.

Canned Hams

50% Power (Medium)
6-8 min. per lb., or
130° internal temperature

Precooked Ham

50% Power (Medium)
10-15 min., per lb., or
130° internal temperature

How to Microwave Precooked or Canned Ham

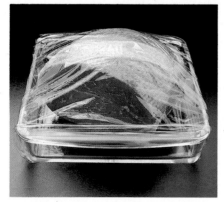

Place ham in baking dish. Cover with vented plastic wrap.

Insert microwave thermometer or probe, if used, so that tip is in center of ham but not touching fat. Do not use a conventional meat thermometer in the microwave oven.

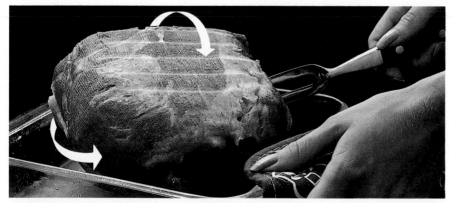

Microwave at 50% power ½ the total time. Turn over, rotate and re-cover ham. Microwave for remaining time, or to internal temperature of 130°.

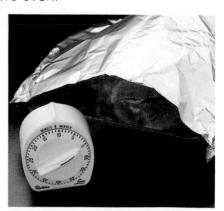

Cover ham with foil, shiny side in; let stand 5 to 10 minutes.

Bacon

There are several ways to microwave bacon. Choose the one that suits your needs and the type of bacon you prefer.

Bacon varies in thickness, number of slices per pound and the amount of salt and sugar used in curing. These factors affect cooking times and methods. Thick slices and home cures take more time. When microwaving several layers of bacon, reduce the time per slice.

Microwaved bacon doesn't curl or spatter; it shrinks less and needs less attention than conventionally fried. Clean-up is easy.

High Power
1 to 6 slices	¾-1 min. per slice
Over 6 slices	½-¾ min. per slice

How To Microwave Bacon

Layer 3 paper towels. Place them directly on the oven floor or on a paper or microwave oven-proof plate.

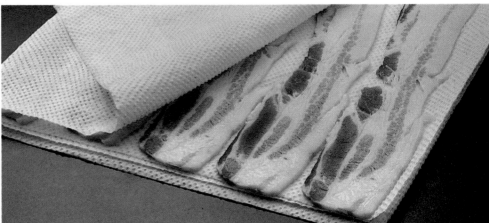

Arrange 1 to 6 strips of bacon on towels and cover with another towel. Microwave and let stand 5 minutes. Paper may develop brown spots and stick slightly if bacon has a high sugar content.

70

Roasting Rack Method

Use a roasting rack or trivet in a baking dish when you wish to save drippings, or if you prefer the broiled type of bacon. Cover bacon with a paper towel before microwaving to absorb spatters.

Let bacon stand 5 minutes after microwaving. It should be removed from the oven while fat is still slightly translucent and bubbly. Bacon cooked on a roasting rack will not be as flat or crisp as bacon cooked on paper towels. Timings in chart are for medium-cooked bacon.

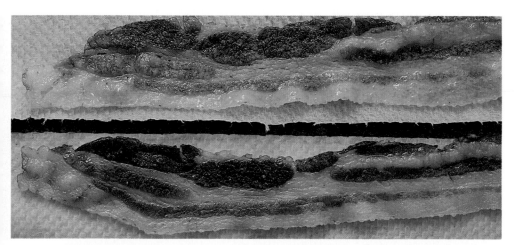

Remove bacon from oven while it still looks slightly underdone. After standing it will be evenly cooked and brown. Microwave bacon on paper towels if you prefer crisp-cooked bacon.

Use a paper towel lined baking dish for several layers of bacon. Cover each with towel. Rotate dish after ½ cooking time.

Sausages

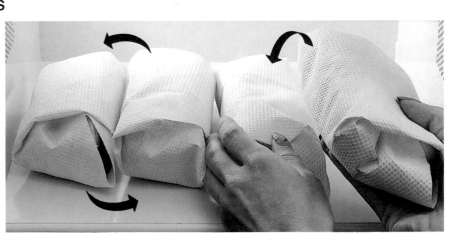

Wieners and frankfurters vary in size. Times in the chart are for medium wieners (10 to 12 per lb.). When heating smaller wieners, check at the minimum time. Wieners and franks are fully cooked and take little time to heat.

Larger sausages, such as bratwurst, knockwurst and Polish sausage are also fully cooked. They take a little longer to heat and should be turned over after ½ the time.

Uncooked breakfast sausage links and patties vary greatly in fat content, which affects the amount of shrinkage. If you use the roasting rack method, you will want a browning agent, since plain microwaved sausage is gray when fully cooked.

Wieners in Buns

High Power

1 wiener	½-¾ min.
2 wieners	¾-1¼ min.
4 wieners	1¾-2¾ min.

How to Microwave Wieners

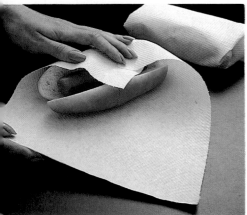

Place wiener in bun. Wrap in paper napkin or towel. Microwave at High according to chart.

Rearrange once when heating 4 wieners by moving outside ones to center. When wieners are heated without buns, times are slightly shorter.

How to Microwave Sausage Patties or Links

Roasting rack method. Place rack in 12×8-in. baking dish. Arrange sausage on rack. Brush with equal parts bouquet sauce and water. Cover with wax paper. Microwave on first side. Turn over. Brush with sauce mixture. Cover. Microwave second side.

Browning dish method. Preheat browning dish as manufacturer directs. Place sausage in dish. Microwave first side. Turn sausage over. Microwave second side.

High Power

Patties, 2-oz., 3-in. diameter			Sausage Links			Brown & Serve Links		
Quantity	1st side Minutes	2nd side Minutes	Quantity	1st side Minutes	2nd side Minutes	Quantity	1st side Minutes	2nd side Minutes
Rack Method			Rack Method			Rack Method		
2	1 - 1½	2 - 2½	2	1	1 - 1½	2	½	½ - 1
4	1½ - 2	2½ - 3	4	1	1 - 1½	4	½	1
8	3 - 3½	4 - 4½	8	1½ - 2	2	8	1	1
Browning Dish			Browning Dish			Browning Dish		
2	½	1	2	½	½ - 1	2	¼	¼ - ½
4	1½	1½ - 2	4	½ - 1	1	4	½	½
8	2	2½ - 3	8	1 - 1½	1½	8	½	½ - ¾

Wiener & Bean Pot Casserole

½ cup chopped onions
1 clove garlic, crushed
2 tablespoons butter or
    margarine
1 pkg. wieners (12 to 16-oz.)
    cut in quarters
1 can (16-oz.) baked beans
1 can (16-oz.) lima beans,
    drained

1 can (16-oz.) kidney beans,
    drained
½ cup brown sugar
½ cup catsup
1 tablespoon prepared
    mustard
½ teaspoon salt
¼ teaspoon pepper

Serves 4 to 6

Combine onions, garlic and butter in 3-qt. casserole. Microwave at High 1 to 2 minutes, until onions are soft and translucent. Add remaining ingredients. Push wieners to bottom of dish so they are buried under beans. Cover. Microwave 13 to 15 minutes, until heated through, stirring after ½ the time.

Shield wieners by pushing ▶
them underneath beans.

Poultry

Chicken is one of our best and most economical sources of protein. Most Americans eat it at least once a week. Chicken is an ideal food for microwaving; it's tender and juicy, responds to a variety of flavoring and cooks in fractions of the conventional time. The juices rendered are highly nutritious, and should be saved for sauces, soups or enriching vegetables.

Cornish hens and chicken pieces microwave so quickly they do not have time to crisp and brown. Use a browning agent or a crumb coating, or add flavor and eye appeal by cooking in a colorful sauce.

Selecting, Storing, Freezing & Defrosting Chicken

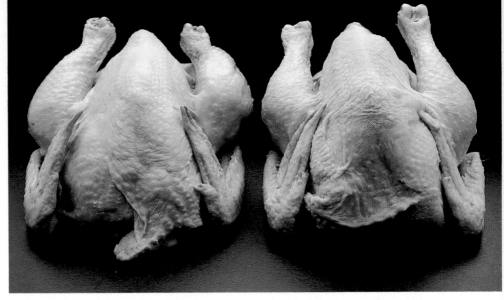

Select meaty young chickens with thin, smooth skins. Scrawny birds with thick, pitted skin and dark yellow fat will be tough.

How to Defrost Chicken Quarters or Pieces

Chicken spoils rapidly. It can be stored in its original package, but should be used the day you buy it, or on the following day. If you don't intend to use it within that time, freeze it as soon as you bring it home.

Wash chicken before cooking it. Large pores encourage bacteria growth. Most chicken fat is concentrated under the skin; you can reduce calories by removing skin and fat. Cook skinned chicken with crumbs or a browning agent, or cook in a colorful sauce.

Chicken	Min./lb. 50%	Min./lb. 30%
Whole	2½-5	7-9
Quarters	4½-5½	6-8
Pieces	2-4½	6-8

Defrost times are given for two power levels; 50% (Medium) and 30% (Low).

Remove twist ties. Place unopened plastic or paper-wrapped package in oven. Defrost for ½ the total time.

Turn package over. Defrost for ¼ the total time.

How to Defrost a Whole Chicken

Remove twist tie if chicken is in plastic bag. Place package in oven. Defrost for ½ of time.

Shield ends of legs and any warm spots with small pieces of foil.

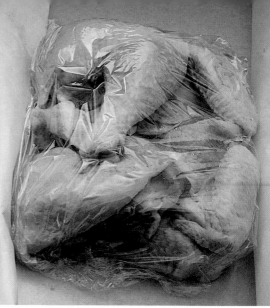

Freeze chicken parts or whole chickens in the original package for storage up to 2 weeks. When buying chicken for the freezer, choose one with a minimum of moisture in the package.

Rewrap chicken in wax-coated freezer paper for longer storage, they will keep 6 to 12 months.

Unwrap and separate pieces. Arrange in dish with meatiest parts to outside.

Microwave remaining time. Let stand 5 minutes or until chicken feels soft but still cold.

Wash chicken parts in cold water before using.

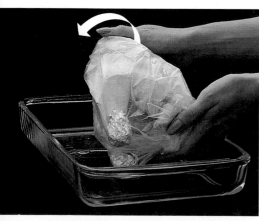

Turn chicken over, it may be left in bag or placed in dish. Defrost for second ½ of time.

Loosen giblets and wings. Let chicken stand 5 minutes.

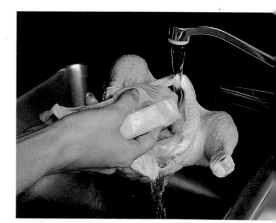

Remove giblets; rinse cavity with cold water until it is no longer icy.

How to Microwave Plain Chicken

Plain microwaved chicken is similar to poached, but it steams quickly in its own natural juices without additional liquid. Use it in any recipe calling for cooked chicken: main dishes, salads or sandwiches. To minimize calories, remove skin and excess fat before cooking.

Arrange chicken with meatiest parts to outside of dish. If desired, season with pinch of parsley, tarragon or crumbled bay leaf.

Cover tightly with plastic wrap vented at one edge of dish (see page 12). Microwave at High for ½ the cooking time.

Rearrange chicken so that areas which appear less cooked are to outside of dish. Replace plastic wrap and microwave remaining time.

How to Microwave Sauce-Coated Chicken

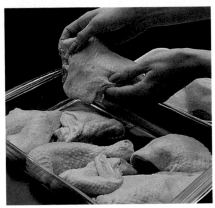

Arrange chicken with meatiest portions to outside of dish.

Brush with barbecue or other sauce.

Cover with wax paper. Microwave at High for ½ the total cooking time.

Rearrange pieces so that less cooked parts are brought to outside of dish.

Brush with sauce again and re-cover with wax paper.

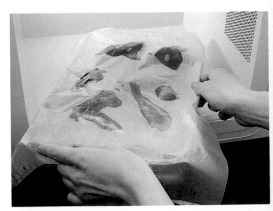

Microwave remaining ½ of time or until tender.

High Power

1 piece (leg, breast or thigh)	2½-4½ min.
2 pieces	6-6½ min.
3 pieces	7½-8½ min.
4 pieces	9-10 min.
1 quarter	7½-9 min.
2 quarters	13-13½ min.
1 chicken, cut up	5½-7½ min. per lb.

Test chicken for doneness. Meat next to the bone should be fork-tender with no tinge of pink. The juices should run clear.

Sauce-Coated Variations

Oriental Chicken. Marinate in soy or teriyaki sauce for 15 minutes. Brush with marinade during microwaving, if desired.

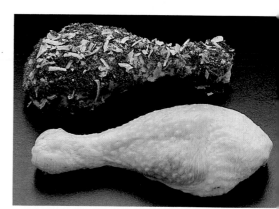

Onion-Dipped Chicken. Turn chicken pieces in dry onion or onion-mushroom soup mix before arranging them in baking dish.

Sunday Chicken Bake

This easy, dressed-up chicken dinner is microwaved at 50% power because sour cream curdles at high temperatures. Skinning the chicken allows more flavor to be absorbed by the meat.

4 servings cooked rice, page 122
4 half chicken breasts, boned and skinned
1 can (10¾-oz.) cream of mushroom soup, undiluted
8 oz. fresh mushrooms, sliced
1 cup dairy sour cream
½ cup dry sherry
1 tablespoon chopped, candied ginger
2 tablespoons snipped fresh parsley

Serves 4

How to Microwave Sunday Chicken Bake

Microwave rice; set aside covered. Arrange chicken breasts in 8×8-in. dish.

Combine rest of ingredients in small bowl. Pour over chicken. Cover with vented plastic wrap.

Microwave at 50% power (Medium) for 15 minutes. Turn chicken over. Re-cover. Microwave 10 to 20 minutes, until chicken is fork tender.

Crispy Coated Chicken

1 2½ to 3½-lb. broiler-fryer, quartered or cut in pieces

Coating mixture:

1 cup corn flake crumbs
6 tablespoons grated
   Parmesan cheese
2 teaspoons parsley flakes
1 small clove garlic, crushed
½ teaspoon salt
   Dash pepper

Dipping mixture:

¼ cup butter
2 eggs, beaten

High Power

5½-8 minutes per pound

How to Microwave Crispy Coated Chicken

Skin chicken and remove excess fat.

Combine coating ingredients in a 1-qt. casserole.

Melt butter at High ¾ to 1 minute. Stir into beaten eggs.

Dip chicken in egg mixture, then turn in crumbs to coat well.

Arrange chicken over rice on serving platter. Spoon some of sauce onto chicken. Serve rest in gravy boat. Garnish with paprika and chopped olives.

Arrange in 12x8-in. dish with bony sides down and thick pieces to outside of dish. Cover with wax paper. Microwave ½ the time.

Rearrange chicken so that areas which are least cooked come to outside of dish. Discard wax paper. Microwave for second ½ of time.

Whole Chickens

A whole chicken turns a light golden brown during micro-waving. For richer color, you can brush the chicken with glaze half way through cooking, or use a browning sauce as suggested below. Because chicken skin is very fatty, dilute the bouquet sauce with butter and rub it into the skin. Brushed-on liquid beads up and streaks.

High Power, 3 min.
50% Power, 10-12 min./lb.

How to Microwave a Whole Chicken

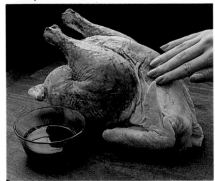

Dry chicken thoroughly. Rub a mixture of equal parts brown bouquet sauce and melted butter into skin.

Place chicken breast side down in baking dish. Micro-wave at High 3 minutes. Re-duce power to 50%. Micro-wave for ½ of time.

Turn chicken breast side up. Microwave second ½ of time, or until legs move easily and meat around bone is done.

Rice Stuffing

2 tablespoons butter or
   margarine
½ cup sliced brazil nuts or
   almonds
½ cup finely chopped celery
¼ cup chopped onion
1½ cups cooked rice
¼ cup raisins

2 teaspoons parsley flakes
½ teaspoon salt
⅛ teaspoon rosemary
⅛ teaspoon sage
⅛ teaspoon thyme
⅛ teaspoon pepper

Makes 4 servings

Combine butter, nuts, celery and onion in 1-qt. casserole. Cover. Microwave 2 to 4 minutes at High, or until celery is tender and onions are translucent. Set aside. In small bowl, mix together re-maining ingredients; stir into nut mixture. Use to stuff 4 cornish hens or a 3 to 4-lb. chicken. To serve as a side dish, microwave covered 1 to 2 minutes on High, or until heated through.

Cornish Game Hens

Cornish hens are often found as a supermarket special, and make a "company" meal for guests or family. Due to their low fat content, a browning agent is needed for color.

Defrosting
50% Power (Medium)
5-7 min. per lb.

30% Power (Low)
7-9 min. per lb.

Cooking
High Power
5½-8 min. per lb.

Pictured on pages 74 & 75.

How to Defrost Cornish Game Hens

Unwrap hens. Place in baking dish. Cover with wax paper. Defrost for ½ of time.

Turn over. When doing several hens, turn so sides which were to edge of dish are in center.

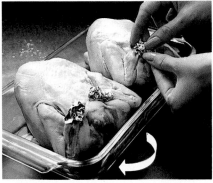

Shield tips of wings and legs if needed. Rotate dish ½ turn. Defrost remaining time.

How to Microwave Cornish Game Hens

Place breast side down in baking dish. Brush with mixture of equal parts bouquet sauce and water.

Cover with wax paper. Microwave at High for ¼ the time. Rotate dish ½ turn.

Microwave for ¼ the time. Turn breast side up so sides which were to edge of dish are in center.

Brush with bouquet mixture. Microwave ¼ the time. Rotate dish ½ turn.

Microwave remaining time until leg moves freely and juices from inner thigh run clear.

Let stand, covered, 5 to 10 minutes to complete cooking.

Defrosting Turkey and Turkey Parts

While turkey may not be an everyday food, defrosting turkey in the microwave oven is truly convenient when you do serve it. Whole turkey and parts may be left in the original wrappings for the first half of defrosting, but it is easier to detect overly defrosted areas if the meat is unwrapped right from the start.

Whole Turkey

50% Power (Medium)
3½-5½ min. per lb.

30% Power (Low)
5½-8 min. per lb.

How to Defrost Whole Turkey

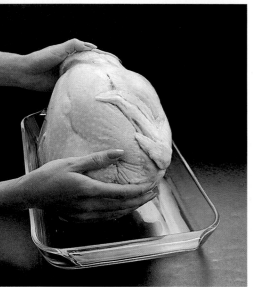

Place unwrapped turkey in baking dish, breast side down. Defrost for ¼ the total time.

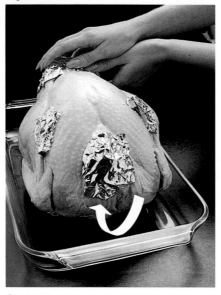

Shield any warm spots with foil. Turn turkey breast side up. Defrost for ¼ the time.

Turn turkey over. Shield leg and wing tips and any warm or brown areas.

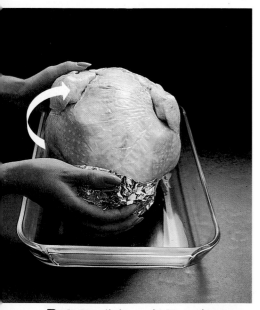

Rotate dish so legs point to opposite side of oven. Defrost for ¼ the time. Turn over again.

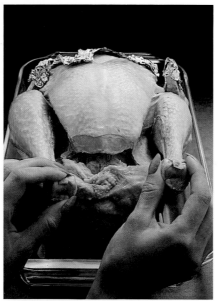

Defrost remaining time. Spread legs and wings from body. Loosen giblets.

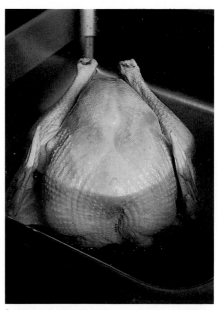

Let turkey stand in cool water 20 to 30 minutes, or until giblets and neck can be removed and interior is cool but not icy.

Turkey Parts

50% Power (Medium)
3-6 min. per lb.

30% Power (Low)
7-9½ min. per lb.

How to Defrost Turkey Breast

Place unwrapped turkey breast in baking dish, breast side down. Defrost for ½ the time.

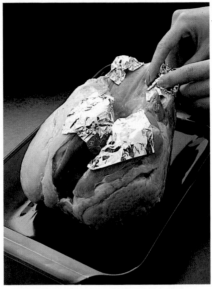

Shield warm areas. Turn breast side up. Defrost remaining time. Rinse in cool water.

Let stand 5 to 10 minutes, or until cavity is no longer icy.

How to Defrost Turkey Legs

Separate pieces, if possible. Arrange in baking dish with meaty parts to outside of dish. Defrost for ½ the time.

Shield any warm areas, Turn pieces over, separating if necessary. Defrost for remaining time, until surface is pliable but not hot.

Rinse in cool water. Let stand 5 minutes, or until meat can be pierced to the bone with a fork.

Fish & Seafood

Microwaving is an excellent way of preparing fish and sea-food. Quick, moist cooking and minimal handling is best for these delicate foods which dry out, toughen or break apart easily.

Many microwave oven owners believe that microwaved fish tastes far less "fishy" than conventionally cooked. You may notice a slight fishy odor when defrosting and microwaving frozen fish, but it seems to disappear after cooking.

Be careful not to overcook fish and seafood. They are done as soon as they flake or lose their translucent appearance.

50% Power (Medium)
3-5 min. per lb.

30% Power (Low)
6½-8½ min. per lb.

How to Defrost Fish Fillets, Steaks & Small Whole Fish

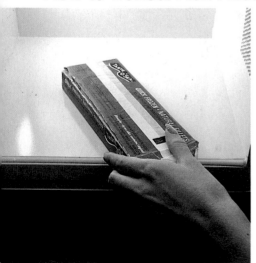

Open package. If pieces can be separated, place them in dish in which they will be cooked. Place dish or package in oven.

Defrost for ½ the time. Separate, rearrange or turn fish over so less defrosted parts are brought to top and outside of dish.

Defrost remaining time, or until fish is pliable on outside but icy in center or thick areas. Let stand 5 minutes. Rinse well.

How to Microwave Salmon or Halibut Steaks 50% Power (Medium), 10-13 min. per lb.

Arrange steaks in baking dish. Melt 2 tablespoons butter for each pound of fish. Add 1 teaspoon lemon juice. Brush on steaks.

Cover with vented plastic wrap. Microwave at 50% power (Medium) for ½ the cooking time.

Turn steaks over. Brush with lemon-butter; cover. Microwave remaining time until fish flakes easily.

Fish Fillets

Fish fillets can be microwaved at High power in most ovens, but occasionally small areas may pop. This does not dry out or toughen the fish, nor does it affect the flavor. If popping is a problem in your oven, use the 50% power level for best results.

Poached Fish

High Power
5-7 min. per lb.

50% Power (Medium)
10-13 min. per lb.

Steamed Fish

High Power
5½-8 min. per lb.

50% Power (Medium)
11-14 min. per lb.

How to Microwave Poached Fish Fillets

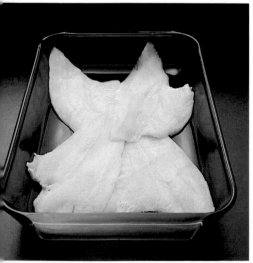

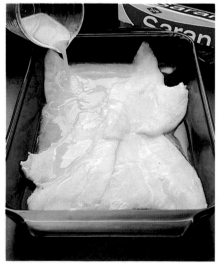

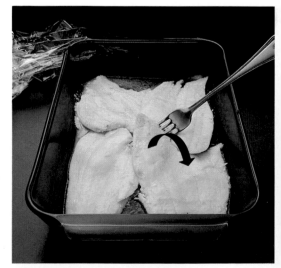

Arrange fillets in baking dish with thickest portions to the outside. Overlap thin areas in center of dish.

Pour on lemon juice or melted butter, or sprinkle with seasonings, if desired. Cover with vented plastic wrap. Microwave for ½ the time.

Reverse overlapping thin areas and move less cooked portions to outside of dish. Recover. Microwave remaining time or until fish flakes easily.

Tuna Casseroles

The basic procedure shown here can be used to microwave any casserole which calls for cooked or canned meat, poultry or fish. Since all the ingredients are cooked, microwave just long enough to heat the dish through.

Tuna & Rice Casserole

1 pkg. (3-oz.) cream cheese
1 can (10¾-oz.) cream of
    mushroom soup, undiluted
2 cups cooked rice
1 can (6½ to 7-oz.) tuna,
    drained
1 can (4-oz.) mushroom
    stems and pieces, drained
¼ cup chopped green onions
1 tablespoon parsley
⅛ teaspoon pepper
¼ cup Parmesan cheese
    Paprika

Serves 4 to 6

Soften cream cheese in a 2-qt. casserole 20 to 25 seconds at High. Blend in soup. Stir in rice, tuna, mushrooms, onions, parsley and pepper. Microwave at High 5 minutes. Stir well. Sprinkle with cheese and paprika. Microwave 4 to 6 minutes, until heated through.

Curried Tuna-Noodle Casserole

1 can (10¾-oz.) cream of
    celery soup, undiluted
½ cup milk
½ teaspoon curry powder
1 can (6½ to 7-oz.) tuna,
    drained
3 cups (6-oz.) cooked noodles
1 cup thinly sliced celery
¾ cup raisins
½ cup slivered almonds
1 can (3-oz.) French fried
    onion rings, divided

Serves 4 to 6

Combine soup, milk and curry powder in 2-qt. casserole. Stir in tuna, noodles, celery, raisins, almonds and ½ the onion rings. Microwave at High 5 minutes. Stir well. Sprinkle on remaining onion rings. Microwave 4 to 6 minutes, until heated through.

How to Microwave Tuna Casseroles

Steamed fish is microwaved the same as poached but should be covered with a dampened paper towel instead of plastic wrap.

Combine all ingredients except topping, in the order given. Microwave for ½ the time. Stir. Layered casseroles should be rotated after ½ the time.

Sprinkle on topping, which gives the casserole an attractive finish. Microwave remaining time, until well heated.

Scallops Au Gratin

1 lb. cooked scallops, below, drained
1 cup white sauce, page 102
1½ tablespoons butter or margarine
2 tablespoons seasoned bread crumbs
1 to 2 tablespoons grated Parmesan cheese

Serves 4

Combine scallops and white sauce. Spoon into 4 ramekins or scallop shells. In 1-cup measure, melt butter at High 15 to 45 seconds. Stir in bread crumbs. Sprinkle over scallops; top with cheese. Microwave 1½ to 2½ minutes, rotating once, until heated.

How to Defrost Scallops

50% Power (Medium), 3½-5½ min. per lb.
30% Power (Low), 5-7½ min. per lb.

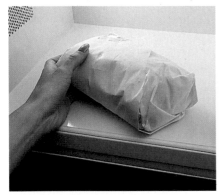

Place paper or plastic package in oven. If scallops are frozen in a can, remove them and place in baking dish. Defrost for ½ the time.

Break up block of scallops with fork. Spread in single layer in baking dish. Defrost remaining time.

Rinse in cool water. Let stand 1½ to 2 minutes to complete defrosting. Scallops should feel cool and soft.

How to Microwave Scallops High Power, 3½-5 min. per lb.

Spread scallops in a single layer in 8×8-in. dish. Cover with vented plastic wrap.

Microwave at High for ½ the cooking time. Stir to rearrange. Microwave remaining time or until scallops are opaque.

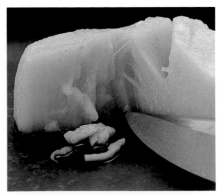

Let stand 1 minute. Test for doneness by cutting a scallop. Inside texture should be flaky.

Saucy Shrimp

1 lb. peeled, deveined, quick-cooking shrimp defrosted, below, drained
1 can (16-oz.) tomato sauce
¾ cup chopped green pepper (1 small)
¾ cup chopped onion (1 small)
1½ tablespoons parsley flakes
⅛ teaspoon garlic powder

Serves 4

Combine all ingredients in a 12×8-in. dish; mix well. Arrange shrimp in single layer. Cover with plastic wrap. Microwave at High 6½ to 9 minutes, stirring once, until shrimp are opaque. Let stand, covered, 1 to 2 minutes. Serve over rice, if desired.

How to Defrost Shrimp

50% Power (Medium), 3-4½ min. per lb.
30% Power (Low), 4-6½ min. per lb.

Separate peeled, deveined, quick-cooking shrimp, if possible. Place in single layer in baking dish.

Defrost for ½ the time. Break up and stir to rearrange. Defrost remaining time.

Rinse in cool water. Let stand 2 minutes. Shrimp should be cool, soft and translucent.

How to Microwave Shrimp

High Power, 3½-5 min. per lb.

Arrange shrimp in single layer in baking dish. Cover with vented plastic wrap.

Microwave for ½ the time. Stir to rearrange so less cooked shrimp are near outside of dish. Cover.

Microwave remaining time until shrimp turn pink and opaque. Let stand, covered, 1 to 2 minutes.

91

Eggs

Eggs illustrate one difference between conventional and microwave cooking. When you poach or shirr an egg conventionally, it cooks first in the outer, or white portion. This is also true of boiled eggs, which must always be cooked conventionally.

The opposite is true in microwaving. Since an egg yolk contains more fat than the white, it attracts more energy. If you microwave an egg until the white is set, the yolk will toughen. Standing time is necessary to cook the white completely without hardening the yolk. When yolks and whites are mixed together, microwaving is even, but standing time is still used to cook eggs delicately.

Never microwave an egg in its shell. Steam builds up inside and egg will burst.

Browning Dish Bacon and Eggs

Preheat browning dish 2 minutes at High. Cut 2 strips of bacon in half. Place them against sides of dish; microwave 2 minutes. Break 2 eggs into dish, baste with bacon fat. Remove and drain bacon on paper towel. Cover dish; microwave 15 to 30 seconds. Let eggs stand 2 to 3 minutes, until set.

Scrambled Eggs

Microwave-scrambled eggs are fluffier and have more volume than conventionally-scrambled. You can microwave and serve or eat them from the same dish. Butter suggested in these directions is for flavor only; it isn't needed to prevent sticking, so if you're calorie conscious, you can omit it and also substitute water for milk.

Tastes differ in scrambled eggs; you may prefer them more or less firm. Remove them from the oven while they still look underdone. Overcooking makes them rubbery. If, after standing, they are not done to your satisfaction, microwave them a few seconds longer.

High Power

Eggs	Butter	Milk	Time
1	1 tbsp.	1 tbsp.	35-45 sec.
2	1 tbsp.	2 tbsp.	1¼-1¾ min.
4	1 tbsp.	2 tbsp.	2-3 min.
6	2 tbsp.	¼ cup	3¼-4¼ min.
10	3 tbsp.	½ cup	5¼-6½ min.

How to Microwave Scrambled Eggs

Place butter in serving dish or casserole. Microwave 30 seconds at High until butter melts.

Add eggs and milk. Scramble with a fork. Microwave at High for about half the cooking time.

Open the oven door. Eggs are beginning to set around the edges, where they receive most energy.

Break up set parts and push them to center of dish. Cook remaining time, stirring once or twice more.

Remove eggs from oven while they are still soft and moist. Let them stand 1 to 4 minutes.

Eggs continue to cook and will be set after standing. Stir eggs before serving.

Sunday Brunch Eggs

Dice 1 slice bacon per egg. Microwave at High 30 seconds per slice. Chop 1 tablespoon each mushroom and green onion. Add to bacon.

Microwave 30 seconds more per slice. Drain off fat. Add eggs and milk; scramble. Microwave and stir as directed above. Increase time if necessary.

Serve for a special breakfast. Try different flavor combinations, such as chopped ham, green pepper and tomato for Western style eggs.

Poached Eggs

Eggs are easy to poach in the microwave oven if you observe these simple rules: Bring water and vinegar to a full boil before adding the egg. Reduce the power level so egg will poach gently. Standing time is important. It allows the white to set without overcooking the yolk. After standing, slip the egg into a slotted spoon to drain. If the bottom is not set to your satisfaction, turn egg over into custard cup and microwave a few seconds more.

50% Power (Medium)

1 egg	45 sec. to 1 min. 20 sec.
2 eggs	1 min. 5 sec. to 1 min. 35 sec.
4 eggs	2 min. 15 sec. to 3 min. 15 sec.

How to Microwave Poached Eggs

Measure 2 tablespoons water and ¼ teaspoon vinegar into 6-oz. custard cup. (One per egg.) Cover with plastic wrap. Bring to a boil at High power, 30 to 40 seconds per cup.

Break large eggs into cups. Cover. Microwave at 50% power until most of the white is opaque but not set. When poaching more than 1 egg, rotate dishes every 45 seconds.

Let stand 2 to 3 minutes. Shaking cups gently once or twice during standing helps set white. Do not remove cover until standing time is completed.

Eggs Florentine. Serve poached eggs on a bed of spinach, garnished with crumbled crisp bacon.

Puffy Omelet

4 large eggs
¼ cup milk
½ teaspoon salt
¼ teaspoon baking powder
⅛ teaspoon pepper
1 tablespoon butter or
   margarine

Serves 2 to 4

Filling:
One or more of the following:
Shredded cheese; crumbled
crisp bacon; sliced cooked
mushrooms; chopped ham;
chopped green pepper;
chopped green onion; sautéed
onion slices; chopped tomato;
diced, cooked potato;
shredded chipped beef;
chopped cooked shrimp.

How to Microwave a Puffy Omelet

Separate eggs, placing whites in 1-qt. mixing bowl and yolks in smaller bowl.

Beat whites until stiff but not dry. Blend together yolks, milk, salt, baking powder and pepper.

Fold yolk mixture into beaten egg whites gently, using rubber spatula.

Melt butter in 9-in. pie plate at High 30 to 45 seconds. Pour in eggs. Microwave at 50% power 3 to 5 minutes until partially set.

Lift edges with spatula so uncooked portion spreads evenly. Microwave 2½ to 4½ minutes, until center is almost set.

Sprinkle desired filling over ½ of omelet. Loosen omelet with spatula and fold in half. Gently slide onto serving plate.

Cheese

High fat content of cheese attracts microwave energy. Add to casseroles toward the end of cooking.

American-Swiss Fondue

1 clove garlic, halved
8 oz. grated cheddar cheese
8 oz. grated Swiss cheese
3 tablespoons flour
    Dash nutmeg
1 cup dry white wine
    Cubes of crusty French bread

Serves 4

Rub a 2-qt. casserole with cut garlic. Discard. Shake cheese, flour and nutmeg together in small bag. Measure wine into casserole. Microwave at 50% power (Medium) 3 to 4 minutes, until wine is hot but not boiling.

Stir in cheese mixture. Microwave 6 to 8 minutes, until smooth, stirring vigorously every 2 minutes with a fork or wire whip. Serve hot with bread cubes for dipping.

Macaroni & Cheese

1 pkg. (7-oz.) elbow
    macaroni
3 tablespoons butter or
    margarine
3 tablespoons flour
1 teaspoon salt
½ teaspoon dry mustard
¼ teaspoon pepper
1½ cups milk
2 cups grated cheese

Serves 6

Photo directions opposite.

Grilled Cheese Sandwiches

This sandwich can be made outside the oven; heat from the browning dish is sufficient to brown the bread and melt the cheese.

For each sandwich:

2 slices bread
  Butter or margarine

2 slices processed cheese
  (American, Swiss, cheddar)

Variations:

Spread ¼ teaspoon prepared mustard between cheese slices. Substitute 1 slice ham for 1 slice cheese.

How to Microwave Grilled Cheese Sandwiches

Preheat browning dish 4 to 5 minutes or browning grill 6½ to 7½ minutes at High power.

Place cheese between bread slices. Butter outside of sandwich on both sides. Place 1 or 2 sandwiches in preheated dish.

Flatten slightly with spatula. Let stand 15 to 20 seconds. Turn over; let stand 20 to 25 seconds. If necessary, microwave 15 to 25 seconds to finish melting cheese.

How to Microwave Macaroni & Cheese

Cook macaroni conventionally. Drain; set aside. Melt butter in 2 qt. casserole at High power, 40 to 55 seconds. Stir in flour and seasonings until smooth.

Microwave 30 to 45 seconds until heated. Blend in milk smoothly. Microwave 4½ to 5½ minutes until thickened, stirring every minute.

Stir in cheese until melted, microwaving 15 to 20 seconds, if needed. Mix in macaroni well. Microwave 5 to 6 minutes to heat through, stirring once.

Soups

Many of your favorite soup recipes can be microwaved with no change other than a shorter cooking time. If the recipe calls for uncooked rice or pasta, the soup must be cooked long enough to soften these ingredients. Soups made with dried beans or peas can be microwaved, but require advanced techniques. As a beginner, substitute canned beans for ease and speed.

French Onion Soup

4 to 5 large onions, sliced
¼ cup butter or margarine
1 can (10¾-oz.) chicken broth
1 can (10¾-oz.) beef broth
    Water
    Toasted French bread slices
8 oz. shredded Swiss cheese
¼ cup grated Parmesan
    cheese

Serves 4

How to Microwave French Onion Soup

Combine onions and butter in a 3-qt. casserole. Cover. Microwave at High 6½ to 8½ minutes, or until the onions are soft and translucent.

Pour chicken and beef broth into 4-cup measure. Add water to make 1-qt. Stir into onions. Cover. Microwave 4 to 6 minutes until heated through.

Ladle soup into 4 individual casseroles. Top with bread slices to cover. Sprinkle with cheeses. Microwave 5½ to 7½ minutes, until cheese melts. Rearrange dishes once or twice.

98

Summary Vegetable Soup

2 tablespoons butter or
  margarine
1 medium onion, sliced
2 carrots, sliced ¼-in. thick
2 medium potatoes, cut in
  ½-in. dice
2 stalks celery, diced
1 qt. chicken broth or 2 cans
  condensed broth diluted
  with water to make 1-qt.
1 tablespoon parsley
½ teaspoon salt
½ teaspoon basil
¼ teaspoon crushed rosemary
1 tomato, peeled and cut in
  chunks
1 cup frozen cut green beans
1 cup frozen peas
1 cup frozen cauliflowerets
1 to 1½ cups coarsely
  shredded lettuce

Makes eight 1-cup servings

Combine butter and onion in
3-qt. casserole. Microwave at
High 1½ to 2 minutes until
onion is soft. Add carrots, potatoes, celery, broth and seasonings. Cover. Microwave 18
to 20 minutes until vegetables
are almost tender. Stir in tomato
and beans. Cover. Microwave
5 minutes. Stir in peas, cauliflower and lettuce. Cover. Microwave 4 to 5 minutes, until
soup is hot and frozen vegetables are tender.

How to Microwave Canned Soups

Canned soups can be heated in a 4-cup measure, a casserole
or individual serving bowls. If soup is diluted with water, microwave at High. Soups diluted with milk should be heated at 50%
power to prevent overboiling.

Sandwiches

With a microwave oven, a hot sandwich can be ready in about 1 minute. Overheating toughens bread, but a piece of foil on the bottom of the oven will shield the bread from below while the filling protects it from above. Place a paper napkin or towel between bread and foil to absorb excess steam. Toasting the bread before microwaving keeps it from becoming soggy. For other popular sandwiches, see hamburgers, page 58; wieners, page 72 and grilled cheese, page 97.

Open-Face Bacon, Tomato & Cheese Sandwich

For each sandwich:
2 to 3 slices bacon, halved
1 slice bread
2 to 3 slices tomato
1 slice cheese

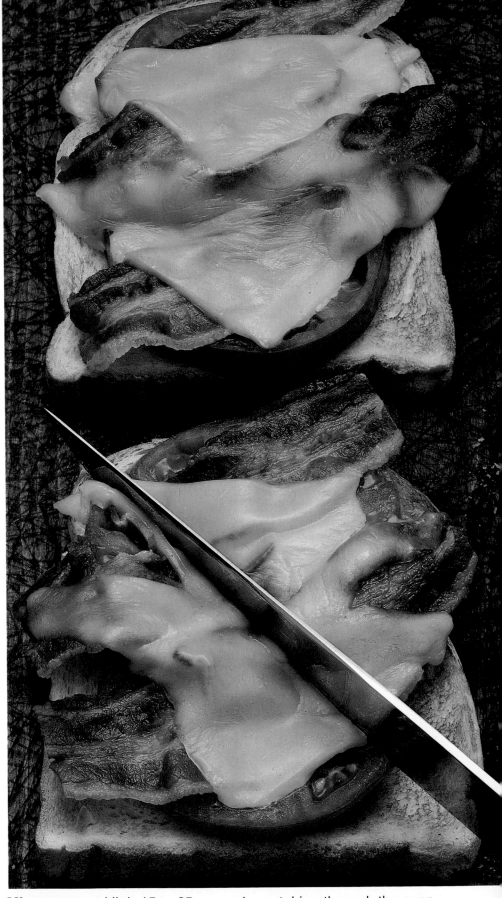

Microwave the bacon, following directions on page 70. While bacon is standing, toast bread; place on paper napkin. Lay thin tomato slices on toast, add bacon and top with cheese. Place sandwich and napkin on foil in oven.

Microwave at High 15 to 35 seconds, watching through the oven door, until cheese melts. Serve whole as a sandwich or cut in fingers to serve as an appetizer.

Hot Turkey or Beef Sandwiches

For each sandwich:
1 to 2 slices bread, toasted
3 oz. thinly sliced cooked
    turkey or beef
1 to 2 tablespoons gravy

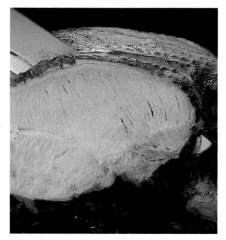

Slice meat about ⅛-in. thick. Several layers of thinly sliced meat heat more evenly than a few thick slices.

Layer meat on a slice of toast. Top with gravy. Arrange on paper napkin and place on foil as directed below. Microwave at High ¾ to 1 minute, until meat is warm. Serve open-faced, or top with second slice of toast and microwave 10 to 15 seconds more.

How to Microwave a Sandwich and Keep a Hard Roll Crisp

Microwave energy drives moisture to the surface of breads. With soft breads and rolls, a paper napkin is sufficient to absorb this moisture, but crusty rolls may soften without shielding.

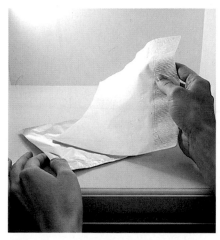

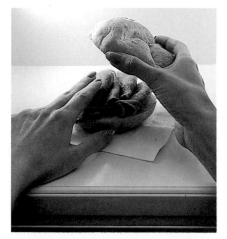

Cut a piece of foil about the same size as the roll. Place it in the oven, shiny side up, lay a paper napkin over the foil.

Layer meat on the bottom half of a crisp roll. Place on napkin. Microwave at High until filling is warm. Cover with top half. Microwave 10 to 15 seconds, until top of roll feels warm.

Sauce

Smooth and easy sauces are another benefit of microwaving. They can be measured, mixed and cooked in the same cup. If the sauce contains milk, be sure to use a large measure to allow for milk's tendency to boil over.

Basic White Sauce

2 tablespoons butter or
 margarine
2 tablespoons flour
¼ teaspoon salt
⅛ teaspoon pepper
1 cup milk

 Makes Approximately 1 cup

Variation:

Cheese Sauce: After microwaving, stir ½ cup shredded cheese into White Sauce.

How to Microwave Basic White Sauce

Melt butter in a 4-cup measure at High, 30 to 50 seconds.

Stir in flour and seasonings until smooth. Blend milk into flour-butter mixture.

Microwave 6 to 8 minutes, until thickened, stirring every minute.

Gravy

Microwaved gravies and sauces need far less stirring than constantly stirred conventional recipes. A wire whip or table fork is the best tool. If you do not have enough meat drippings for gravy, add butter to make ⅓ cup. Do all the measuring in the same cup.

Gravy

1½ cups broth or water
  1 teaspoon beef or chicken bouillon granules, optional
  ⅓ cup flour
  ⅓ cup drippings
    Salt and pepper

Makes 1½ cups

How to Microwave Gravy

Measure broth and bouillon into 4-cup measure. Stir in flour with wire whip until smooth.

Blend meat drippings into broth-flour mixture.

Microwave at High 4 to 6 minutes until thick, stirring twice. Season to taste before serving.

Vegetables

Vegetable Basics

Vegetables retain flavor and nutrients when microwaved. Minerals and vitamins dissolve in water; the less you use, the more nutrients you save. Some vegetables microwave without added moisture. Others need only a little water or butter to provide steam. Learn these vegetable characteristics:

Piece Size. Large pieces take longer to cook than small ones. Keep pieces uniform in size and thickness for even microwaving.

Quantity. Microwaving time increases with the amount of food cooked. Small or medium amounts use energy most efficiently.

Tender Ends. Asparagus buds and broccoli flowerets are more tender than the stalks and need less energy to cook. Arrange them to the center of the dish.

Tight Skins. Prick or cut vegetables cooked in their skins to allow excess steam to escape.

Microwaving Vegetables

Most microwave techniques apply to vegetables. Doneness depends on personal taste. They can be crisp, just tender, or soft. Test after standing and add more time if needed.

Standing time allows vegetables to become tender without losing their texture. If large vegetables are microwaved until the center is tender, the outer portions become mushy.

Cover dish tightly and use a minimum of water. Wrap whole, skinless vegetables in plastic.

Turn over and rearrange large, whole vegetables. If they are stacked in the dish, rearrange from top to bottom and side to center, so all will receive equal energy.

Salt vegetables after cooking, or dissolve salt in cooking water before adding vegetables.

Arrange whole or halved vegetables in a ring, leaving the center open. Rotate both vegetables and dish part way through microwaving for even cooking.

Stir small, loose vegetables from outside to center once or twice to distribute heat.

Baked Potatoes

The potato is an ideal microwave vegetable. Its high moisture content attracts microwave energy, and the natural tight covering holds in steam. The potato's uniform density helps it cook evenly. Times below are for medium size potatoes (5 to 7-oz.).

High Power
1 potato	3-5 min.
2 potatoes	5-7½ min.
3 potatoes	7-10 min.
4 potatoes	10½-12½ min.

How to Microwave Baked Potatoes

Prick well-scrubbed potatoes twice with a fork, so that some steam can escape during microwaving. Place a layer of paper towel on the oven floor to absorb moisture from trapped steam.

Arrange potatoes at least 1 inch apart so that microwave energy can penetrate from all sides.

Twice-Baked Potatoes

For each potato:	Optional:
1 to 2 tablespoons butter	Chopped chives
2 tablespoons milk or sour cream	Shredded cheese
Salt and pepper	Crumbled crisp bacon

After standing time, slice top from each potato; scoop out center. Set shells aside, and mash potatoes with butter and milk. Season; spoon into shells. Chives, cheese or bacon may be mixed into potatoes or used as a topping after reheating. To reheat potatoes before serving, microwave at High about 1 minute per potato. Add an extra ½ minute if potato has been refrigerated.

Turn potatoes over and rearrange them half way through the cooking time. This helps them cook more evenly.

Wrap potatoes in foil, shiny side in, or place them on a counter and cover with a casserole to hold in heat. They will still feel slightly firm, but will complete cooking during 5 to 10 minutes standing time. Potatoes will retain their heat about 45 minutes.

Corn

Microwaving brings out the true flavor of corn, and is the most delicious way of cooking it.

When cooking mature corn in a baking dish, add ¼ cup water, but no salt. Salt toughens corn.

Times are for medium ears.

High Power

2 ears	7-10 min.
4 ears	12-16 min.

How to Microwave Individual Ears

Use corn husk as a natural cover; the silk strips off easily after cooking. Wrap husked ears in plastic wrap to hold in steam. Arrange corn in oven with space between ears.

Microwave at High power. Turn over and rearrange every 4 minutes. Let stand 5 minutes.

How to Microwave a Dish of Corn

Arrange ears in dish large enough to hold them with space between. Add ¼ cup water, if needed. Cover tightly with plastic wrap.

Turn over and rearrange every 4 minutes. Re-cover. Let stand 5 minutes before serving.

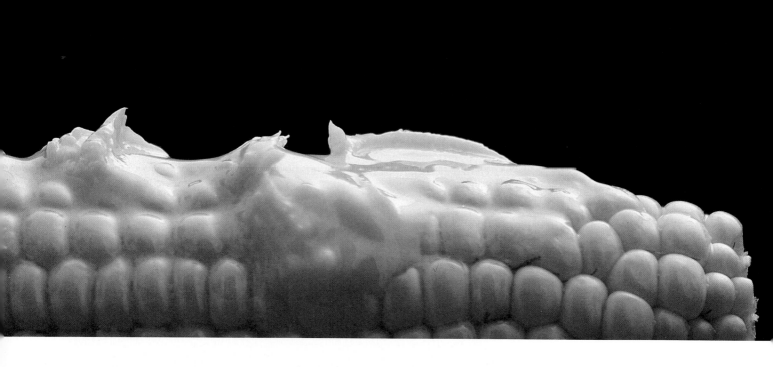

Acorn Squash

Squash is another vegetable which steams in its own natural moisture. If raw squash is difficult to cut, microwave 1 to 2 minutes.

High Power

½ squash	5-8 min.
1 squash	8½-11½ min.
2 squash	13-16 min.

Halve 1½-lb. acorn squash lengthwise. Scoop out seeds. Fit squash halves together again, or cover each with plastic wrap. Microwave for ½ the time. Turn over whole squash or rotate and rearrange halves. Microwave remaining time. Let stand 5 to 10 minutes.

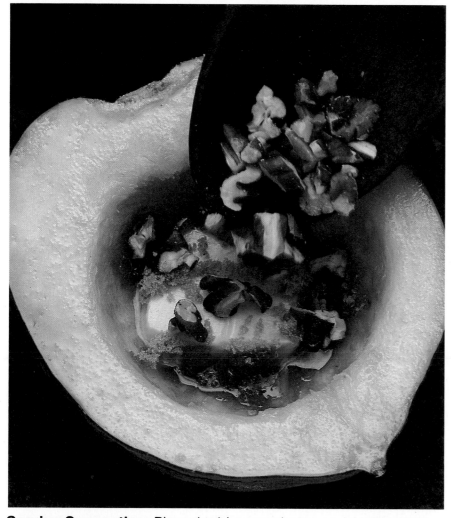

Serving Suggestion: Place 1 tablespoon butter and 1 tablespoon brown sugar in each squash half before standing. Sprinkle with chopped nuts, if desired. Cover with plastic wrap; let stand.

How to Microwave Artichokes   High Power, 2 artichokes: 5½-8½ min.; 4 artichokes: 9½-14½ min.

Trim artichoke 1-in. from top and close to base. Cut off sharp tips of outer leaves. Rinse in water; shake off excess.

Wrap immediately in plastic wrap. Repeat with remaining artichokes. Arrange in oven with space between.

Microwave until lower leaves can be pulled off with slight tug. Rearrange and rotate after ½ the time when cooking more than 2. Let stand 3 minutes, wrapped.

How to Microwave Asparagus   High Power, 1 lb.: 6½-9½ min.

Measure ¼ cup water into 12×8-in. dish. Stir in ¼ teaspoon salt or sugar, if desired. Snap off tough ends from 1 pound of asparagus.

Arrange asparagus spears in dish with buds toward center. Cover with vented plastic wrap. Microwave 4 minutes.

Rearrange so spears on outside of dish are brought to middle. Keep buds toward center of dish. Cover. Microwave remaining time, until tender.

How to Microwave Green Beans   High Power, 2 cups: 12½-17½ min.

Snap enough beans in 1½ to 2-in. pieces to make 2 cups. Place beans and 1 cup water in 9-in. dish or 1½-qt. casserole.

Cover. Microwave, stirring every 4 minutes, until beans lose their raw taste.

Let stand, covered, 3 to 4 minutes to complete cooking and become tender.

How to Microwave Broccoli Spears   High Power, 1½ lbs.: 8-12 min.

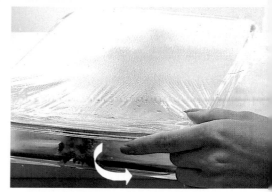

Divide 1 bunch broccoli (1 to 1½-lbs.) into 4 servings. Cut off 1 to 1½-in. from tough ends. Peel skin from about 2-in. of stalks.

Pour ½ cup water into a 10-in. casserole or 12×8-in. baking dish. Arrange broccoli with heads toward center. Cover with plastic wrap.

Microwave, rotating dish ½ turn after ½ the time. Let stand 2 to 3 minutes, covered.

How to Microwave Cabbage Wedges   High Power, 1 lb.: 12½-15½ min.

Cut 1-lb. cabbage into 4 wedges. Arrange like wheel spokes in 10-in. casserole. Add ¼ cup water.

Cover. Microwave, rotating dish after ½ the time. Let stand 2 to 3 minutes, covered.

Wedges may be lined up in 12×8-in. dish, but must be rearranged during cooking.

How to Microwave Sliced Carrots   High Power, 2 cups: 4½-6½ min.

Place 2 cups thinly sliced carrots in a 1-qt. casserole or 9-in. cake dish. Add 2 tablespoons butter or ¼ cup water. Cover.

Microwave, stirring carrots once, if needed.

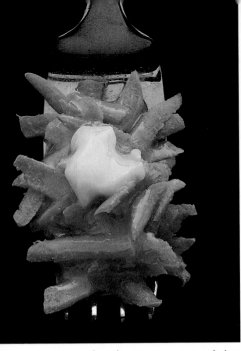

A microwave specialty.

How to Microwave Shredded Carrots (or Zucchini)

High Power, 2 cups
zucchini: 1½-3½ min.
carrots: 3½-6½ min.

Shred enough carrots or zucchini to make 2 cups. Place in 9-in. baking dish with 2 tablespoons butter.

Cover with plastic wrap. Microwave, stirring once after butter melts and before serving.

How to Microwave Whole Cauliflower   High Power, 1 lb.: 5½-7½ min.

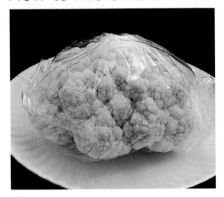

Wash a 1-lb. head of cauliflower. Shake off water. Wrap in plastic wrap. Place on paper plate with sealed edges down.

Microwave 3 minutes. Turn cauliflower over. Microwave remaining time, until head is flexible.

Test floweret stems on under side. They should be almost fork tender. Let stand, covered, 3 minutes to complete cooking.

How to Microwave Cauliflowerets   High Power, 2 cups: 4-7 min.

Place 2 cups cauliflowerets (about ⅔ of 1-lb. head) in a 1½-qt. casserole or 9-in. dish.

Add ¼ cup water. Cover. Microwave, stirring after 3 minutes.

Stems should be just fork-tender. Let stand, covered, 2 minutes to cook completely without overcooking heads.

114

How to Microwave Sliced Celery High Power, 2 cups: 5-8 min.

Slice celery ⅛ to ¼-in. thick to make 2 cups. Place in 1½-qt. casserole or 9-in. dish.

Add 2 tablespoons butter (for flavor) or 2 tablespoons water. Cover with plastic wrap.

Microwave until fork-tender. Stir after 4 minutes. Let stand, covered, 3 minutes.

How to Microwave Sliced Mushrooms High Power, ½ lb.: 3-6 min.

Cut ½-lb. mushrooms in ⅛-in. slices. Microwaving time is directly related to the thickness of slices. Place in 8-in. cake dish with 2 tablespoons butter or margarine. Do not salt; cover.

Microwave, stirring after ½ the time. Serves 2 as a vegetable or 4 as a garnish for steaks.

How to Microwave Whole Onions High Power, 2 onions: 6-8 min.; 4 onions: 9-12 min.

Peel 2½ to 3-in. diameter onions. Remove root end and slice from top, exposing all layers. Place in custard cups or baking dish.

Dot each onion with ½ tea-spoon butter, if desired. They are also delicious plain. Do not salt. Cover tightly. Microwave for ½ the time.

Rotate each onion so side next to outside of dish is turned to-ward center, then rotate dish. Re-cover; microwave remaining time. Let stand 1 to 2 minutes.

115

How to Microwave Peas
High Power, 2 cups: 5-7½ min.

Place 2 cups fresh shelled peas in 1-qt. casserole.

Add 2 tablespoons butter to young peas or ¼ cup water to mature peas. Cover tightly.

Microwave, stirring after ½ the time. Let stand 3 minutes.

How to Microwave Spinach
High Power, 1 lb.: 5-8 min.

 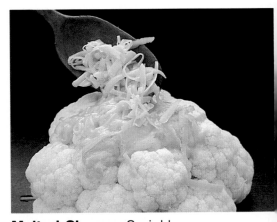

Wash 1-lb. spinach; shake off moisture. Place in 3-qt. casserole. Cover tightly. Microwave 4 minutes.

Stir. Microwave remaining time. Cooking time depends on maturity of spinach.

Toppings to Dress Up Vegetables

White Sauce. Microwave White Sauce, page 102, for creamed cauliflower, peas, onions or carrots, or a mixture of leftover vegetables.

Lemon-Butter Sauce. Melt ¼ cup butter; add 1 tablespoon lemon juice and chopped parsley or dill weed. Excellent with any vegetable.

Melted Cheese. Sprinkle shredded cheese over hot cauliflower or broccoli. Microwave a few seconds if necessary to finish melting.

How to Microwave Tomatoes High Power, 2 tomatoes: 1-3 min.; 4 tomatoes: 2½-4½ min.

Halve 2½-in. diameter tomatoes, keeping them as equal as possible. Times are for medium-ripe tomatoes. Very ripe ones take less time.

Arrange, with space between, in round or rectangular dish. Do not salt. Top with crumbs and Parmesan cheese, if desired. Cover. Microwave ½ the time.

Rotate each tomato half so side near edge of dish comes toward center. Then rotate dish ½ turn. Microwave second ½ of time. Let stand 2 minutes.

How to Microwave Sliced Zucchini High Power, 2 cups: 2½-5 min.

Place 2 cups ¼ to ⅜-in. thick zucchini slices in a 9-in. cake dish or shallow 2-qt. casserole.

Add 2 tablespoons butter for flavor. Cover. Microwave for total time.

Stir Re-cover, let stand 2 to 3 minutes. Serve sprinkled with Parmesan cheese, if desired.

Parmesan Cheese. Try Parmesan cheese with zucchini, tomatoes, beans, asparagus and broccoli. Mix with toasted bread crumbs, if desired.

Toasted Almonds. Sprinkle chopped toasted almonds over celery, beans, asparagus, broccoli or peas.

Crisp Bacon. Microwave a few strips of bacon to crumble over cabbage, beans, potatoes, cauliflower, celery or spinach.

Vegetable Combinations

In each of these combinations, which serves 3 to 4, the first vegetable is microwaved for part of the time before the second is added.

Place the first vegetable in a 9-in. dish or 1½-qt. casserole. Add butter or water. Cover.

Microwave at High first part of time. Stir in second vegetable. Cover. Microwave second time.

Potatoes & Onions

2 medium potatoes, sliced ⅛ to ¼-in. thick (3 minutes*)
1 to 3 tablespoons butter
½ medium onion, sliced ¼ to ⅜-in. thick and broken into rings (3½ to 4½ minutes)

*Stir after 1½ minutes to prevent sticking.

Zucchini & Tomatoes

1 cup ⅛ to ¼-in. thick zucchini slices (2 minutes)
2 tablespoons butter
1 cup ¼-in. tomato wedges (1 to 2½ minutes)

Cauliflowerets & Carrots

1½ cups small to medium cauliflowerets (2 to 3 minutes)
¼ cup water
1 cup ⅛-in. thick carrot slices (2 to 4½ minutes)

Stir-Fried Vegetables

The browning dish gives these combinations, which serve 3 to 4, the flavor and texture of stir-fries, but they are stirred only once. Before using, frozen vegetables should be microwaved in the package 2 to 3 minutes at High, or until they can be separated.

Corn, Peppers & Onions

1 pkg. (10-oz.) frozen corn, separated
⅓ cup ⅜-in. green pepper squares
⅓ cup ⅜-in. onion squares

Time: 4½ to 7½ minutes

Carrots & Celery

1 cup ⅛-in. thick carrot slices
1 cup ¼-in. thick celery slices

Time: 3½ to 5½ minutes

Broccoli & Cauliflowerets

1 to 1⅓ cups broccoli stems (cut in ½ if over 1-in. thick)
1 to 1⅓ cups cauliflowerets (large ones halved or quartered)
¼ cup sliced almonds, optional
1½ teaspoons soy sauce, optional

Time: 4 to 6½ minutes

Pea Pods, Mushrooms & Fresh Bean Sprouts

1 pkg. (6-oz.) frozen pea pods, separated
1 cup ⅛-in. thick fresh mushroom slices
½ cup fresh bean sprouts or ½ cup canned bamboo shoots

Time: 3½ to 6½ minutes

How to Microwave Stir-Fried Vegetables

Preheat browning dish 1 to 2 minutes, depending on size.

Add 2 tablespoons butter or margarine and remaining ingredients. Cover.

Microwave at High, stirring after ½ the cooking time.

Convenience Vegetables

Many frozen vegetable packages now carry microwave directions. If there are no microwave directions, the microwaving time will usually be close to the minimum time for conventional cooking. For example, if instructions require that you bring vegetables to a full boil, then simmer 6 to 8 minutes, microwaving time will probably be 6 minutes from start to finish.

Frozen vegetables in large bags require 2 tablespoons water for 2 cups vegetables. Follow directions for boxed vegetables, opposite, microwaving 5 to 7 minutes. Let stand 2 minutes.

How to Microwave Canned Vegetables

Measure 2 tablespoons liquid from a 1-lb. can of vegetables into a 1-qt. casserole.

Drain vegetables. Add to casserole. Cover.

Microwave at High 3 minutes, stirring after 1½ minutes.

How to Microwave Frozen Vegetable Pouches

Prick pouch with knife tip or fork to vent.

Microwave at High for ½ the time, following manufacturer's microwave directions.

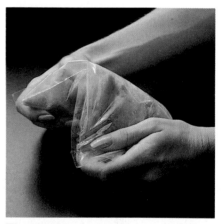

Flex pouch to break up vegetables and distribute heat. Microwave remaining time.

How to Microwave Frozen Boxed Vegetables

Place vegetables in casserole, icy side up.

Add 2 tablespoons water. Cover. Microwave 2 minutes at High.

Break up and stir vegetables. Microwave remaining time.

Rice

Regular long-grain rice is dry grain which needs time to absorb water and soften. Microwaving time is shorter than conventional, but not as much as with moister foods.

High Power & 50% Power

Long Grain Rice	2 servings	4 servings
Casserole	1-1½ qt.	2 qt.
Rice	½ cup	1 cup
Salt	½ teaspoon	1 teaspoon
Water	1 cup	2 cups
Butter	½ teaspoon	1 teaspoon
Start at High Power	3 minutes	5 minutes
Finish at 50% Power	8-10 minutes	11-15 minutes

High Power

Quick-Cooking Rice	2 servings	4 servings
Casserole	1-1½ qt.	2 qt.
Rice	1 cup	2 cups
Salt	¼ teaspoon	½ teaspoon
Water	¾ cup	1⅔ cups
High Power	2½-3½ minutes	6-8 minutes

How to Microwave Rice

Measure rice, salt and butter, margarine or oil, if needed, into casserole.

Stir in hot tap water. Cover. Microwave at High as directed, then change to 50% power if cooking long-grain rice.

Stir long-grain rice. Quick rice needs no stirring. Microwave remaining time. Stir, then let stand, covered, 2 to 4 minutes.

Cereals

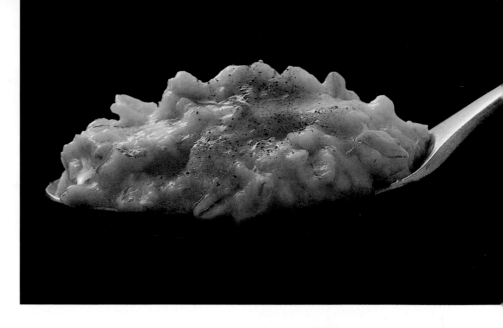

Hot cereals are simple to microwave. All the ingredients are added at the beginning and stirred once during cooking. Best of all, the cereal doesn't stick to the container, so washing up is easy. Be sure to use a bowl large enough to prevent boilover.

High Power

Quick Oatmeal	1 serving	2 servings	4 servings
Bowl Size	1-qt.	1-1½ qt.	2 qt.
Cereal	⅓ cup	⅔ cup	1⅓ cups
Salt	¼ teaspoon	½ teaspoon	¾ teaspoon
Water	¾ cup	1½ cups	3 cups
Time	2-2½ min.	4-5 min.	6-7 min.

Old Fashioned Oatmeal	1 serving	2 servings	4 servings
Bowl Size	1-qt.	1-1½ qt.	2 qt.
Cereal	⅓ cup	⅔ cup	1⅓ cups
Salt	¼ teaspoon	½ teaspoon	1 teaspoon
Water	¾ cup	1⅓ cups	2½ cups
Time	4-6 min.	5-7 min.	8-9 min.

Instant Cream of Wheat	1 serving	2 servings	4 servings
Bowl Size	1 qt.	2 qt.	3 qt.
Cereal	2½ tbsps.	⅓ cup	⅔ cup
Salt	⅛ teaspoon	¼ teaspoon	½ teaspoon
Water	¾ cup	1⅓ cups	2¾ cups
Time	1½-2½ min.	2½-3½ min.	4½-6 min.

Regular Cream of Wheat	1 serving	2 servings	4 servings
Bowl Size	1 qt.	2 qt.	3 qt.
Cereal	2½ tbsps.	⅓ cup	⅔ cup
Salt	⅛ teaspoon	¼ teaspoon	½ teaspoon
Water	1 cup	1¾ cups	3½ cups
Time	4-6 min.	5½-7½ min.	9-12 min.

How to Microwave Hot Cereal

Measure cereal and salt into bowl. Stir in very hot tap water. Microwave ½ the minimum time.

Stir cereal. Microwave remaining time, or until cereal reaches desired thickness. Stir again.

Breads

Quick breads rise higher and bake much faster in a microwave than they do conventionally. Since they do not brown, use colorful batters or toppings to make them look as good as they taste. Boston Brown Bread, pictured at left, is a good example, the recipe is on page 128.

High Power	
1 muffin	25-40 seconds
2 muffins	¾-1½ minutes
4 muffins	1½-2½ minutes
6 muffins	2½-4½ minutes

Rich Muffins

4 tablespoons butter or margarine
1 cup all purpose flour
3 tablespoons sugar
1½ teaspoons baking powder
1 teaspoon grated orange peel
¼ teaspoon salt
⅓ cup milk
1 egg, slightly beaten

Makes 6 to 8 medium muffins

Corn Muffins

¼ cup cooking oil or shortening
½ cup all purpose flour
½ cup yellow corn meal
1 tablespoon sugar
2 teaspoons baking powder
½ teaspoon salt
1 egg
⅓ cup milk

Makes 6 to 8 medium muffins

Bran Muffins

⅓ cup shortening
1 cup bran flakes
⅔ cup milk
1 cup all purpose flour
2 tablespoons sugar
1½ teaspoons baking powder
½ teaspoon salt
¼ cup molasses
1 egg
¼ cup raisins, optional

Makes 10 to 12 medium muffins

How to Microwave Muffins

Melt butter or shortening in custard cup at High, 1 to 1½ minutes. In order given, place remaining ingredients in 2-qt. mixing bowl. Blend in butter.

Place 2 paper baking cups in each custard cup or microwave muffin cup. Fill cups half full, top if desired, page 21. Arrange in oven in ring.

Microwave at High, rotating muffins after ½ the time, until dry on top. (Moist spots will dry on standing.) Remove from cups to wire rack immediately.

Muffins do not brown. Use a topping, if desired. Rich Muffin at right was topped with cinnamon sugar before microwaving.

Fill cups only half full, since microwaved muffins rise higher than conventionally baked.

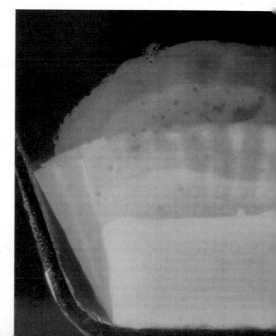

Multiple exposure taken through ▶ the oven door shows how high microwave muffin rises in 20 seconds. Children love to watch them.

Quick Breads

Dense, heavy batters are microwaved at 50% power so they can rise slowly and not overcook on the edges before the center is done. Change the power level to High for the last few minutes to complete cooking.

Banana Bread

1½ cups all purpose flour
¾ cup sugar
½ cup plus 2 tablespoons butter or margarine at room temperature
⅓ cup milk
2 eggs
2 medium small bananas, sliced
1 tablespoon lemon juice or vinegar
1 teaspoon soda
½ teaspoon salt
½ cup chopped nuts, divided

Makes one 8×4 or 9×5-in loaf

NOTE: Loaf dish should be slightly more than half full. If you have extra batter, make 2 or 3 cupcakes. Microwave at High 25 to 40 seconds.

How to Microwave Banana Bread

Place all ingredients except ¼ cup nuts in large bowl in order given. Blend at low speed 15 seconds; beat at medium speed 2 minutes.

Line bottom of loaf dish with wax paper. Spread batter in dish; sprinkle with ¼ cup nuts.

Shield ends of loaf with 2-in. wide strips of foil, covering 1-in. of batter and molding around handles of dish.

Streusel Coffeecake

Cake:

  1 cup all purpose flour
⅔ cup sugar
⅓ cup shortening
1½ teaspoons baking powder
½ teaspoon salt
½ teaspoon vanilla
  2 eggs
½ cup milk, divided

Topping:

Cut together with pastry blender until particles are fine:

½ cup all purpose flour
  2 tablespoons sugar
  2 tablespoons butter or margarine
½ teaspoon cinnamon

Makes one 9-in. round coffeecake

Place all cake ingredients except ¼ cup milk in mixing bowl. Blend at low speed 15 seconds; then beat at medium speed 1 minute. Add remaining ¼ cup milk; beat 1 minute. Line bottom of 9-in. round cake dish with circle of wax paper. Spread batter in dish. Sprinkle with Streusel Topping. Microwave at 50% (Medium) 6 minutes, rotating ½ turn after 3 minutes. Change power level to High. Microwave 3 to 5 minutes, until cake springs back when touched lightly in center.

Place an inverted saucer in oven. Center loaf dish on saucer. Microwave at 50% power (Medium) 9 minutes, rotating ¼ turn every 3 minutes.

Change power level to High. Microwave at High 4 to 7 minutes. Remove foil after 2 minutes.

Check for doneness by looking through bottom of dish. No unbaked batter should appear in center. Let stand 5 to 10 minutes before removing from dish.

127

Dinner Breads

Oatmeal Wheat Bread

    1 cup whole wheat flour
    ½ cup quick-cooking rolled
        oats
    ⅓ cup dark molasses
    ¼ cup shortening
    ¾ cup water
    1 packet dry yeast
    ¼ cup warm water
    1 teaspoon salt
    1½ to 2 cups all purpose flour
        Corn meal
        Milk
        Rolled oats

Makes one loaf

Photo directions opposite

Boston Brown Bread

    ½ cup all purpose flour
    ½ cup whole wheat flour
    ½ cup corn meal
    1 teaspoon soda
    ½ teaspoon salt
    ½ cup raisins
    1 cup buttermilk or sour milk
    ⅓ cup dark molasses
    ¼ cup melted shortening or
        cooking oil

Makes 2 small loaves

How to Microwave Boston Brown Bread

Combine ingredients in mixing bowl; blend well. Line bottom of 2-cup measure with circle of wax paper. Pour in half the batter (about 1⅓ cups). Cover with vented plastic wrap.

Microwave at 50% power (Medium) 6 to 8 minutes, rotating cup ½ turn after 3 minutes. Bread is done when center springs back when touched lightly and no unbaked batter appears on sides of cup.

Cool 5 to 10 minutes. Remove from cup; microwave second loaf with remaining batter. Serve warm. To reheat, place slices on plate. Cover lightly with plastic wrap. Microwave at High 30 to 60 seconds.

How to Microwave Oatmeal Wheat Bread

Combine whole wheat flour, oats, molasses and shortening in mixing bowl. Microwave water at High until boiling. Stir into bowl; cool to warm temperature.

Stir yeast into warm water. Blend into cooled mixture with salt. Stir in flour gradually to make a very stiff dough.

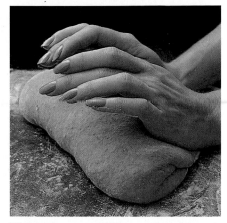

Knead on well-floured surface until smooth, about 5 minutes. Return to greased bowl. Cover.

Let rise in warm place until light and doubled in size, about 1 hour. Shape into ball; cover with bowl. Let rest 15 minutes.

Butter a 10-in. pie plate or microwave baking sheet. Sprinkle with corn meal. Shape dough into a 15-in. strip.

Brush lightly with milk. Roll in oats to coat heavily. Shape into ring on prepared pan. Pinch edges together.

Place greased glass in center. Let rise in warm place until light, 45 to 60 minutes. Sprinkle top lightly with corn meal.

Microwave at 50% power (Medium) 6 minutes, rotating ½ turn after 3 minutes. Change power level to High.

Microwave 4 to 6 minutes, until top springs back when touched lightly. Let stand 10 minutes. Remove bread; cool on rack.

Desserts

Microwaved Mix Cakes

Rich, moist mixes with pudding added are excellent for microwaving. Microwaved cakes rise higher than conventionally baked; fill pans no more than ⅓ to ½ full. Unless you have a special deep-sided microwave cake pan, you may need to make a few cupcakes with the extra batter. Start cake at 50% power to give it a more even top; then finish at High power. Top may be slightly moist when done, but this will evaporate during standing time.

One package makes:	2 8-in. (1-qt.) round layers & 6 cupcakes	2 9-in. (1½-qt.) round layers	2 8×8-in. squares	2½ to 3 dozen cupcakes

Layer Cakes

Start at 50% Power	Finish at High Power
6 minutes	2-5 minutes

Microwave 1 layer at a time.

Cupcakes

Quantity	High Power
1	25-30 seconds
2	¾-1¼ minutes
4*	1½-2 minutes
6*	2-3 minutes

*Rotate and rearrange after ½ the time.

How to Microwave Cake Mixes

Grease dish lightly. If cake is to be turned out, line with wax paper. Prepare mix as directed on package.

Fill dish ⅓ to ½ full. To eliminate air bubbles, cut through batter with spatula. Stir cupcakes with wooden pick.

Microwave layers at 50% (Medium) for slower rising which gives cake a more even surface, as shown through oven window.

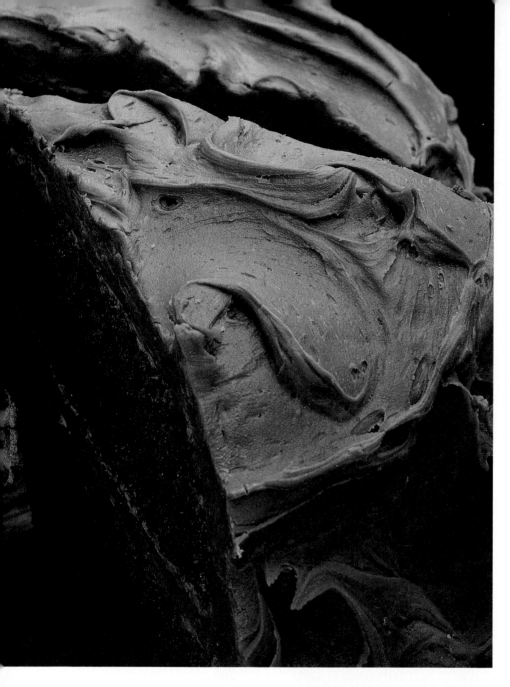

Bundt Cakes

The "ring shape" cake is excellent for microwave. There are a number of microwave bundt pans available. Prepare mix as directed on package and pour into lightly greased pan. You may need to make a few cupcakes if there is too much batter for the pan. Microwave at 50% power (Medium) as directed in chart, rotating cake ¼ turn every 4 or 5 minutes. Then microwave at High for remaining time or until cake starts to pull away from sides of pan. Let stand 10 minutes. Loosen edges carefully with spatula and turn out on wire rack to cool. Freeze or refrigerate cakes at least 1 hour before frosting.

Bundt Cakes

Cake Size	Start at 50% Power	Finish at High Power
14-cup pan	12 min.	4-7 min.
2 8-10-cup pans*	6 min.	3-5 min.

*Microwave 1 at a time.

Rotate ½ turn every 3 minutes. To complete cooking, change to High power after 6 minutes.

Test for doneness by touching cake lightly in center. It should spring back. Slightly moist spots will evaporate.

Let stand directly on counter top 5 to 10 minutes. Turn out of dish, if desired, and frost or top.

Pies

Microwaved pastry is exceptionally tender, flaky and puffy, but it does not brown. Add a few drops of food coloring, or brush pastry with egg yolk before microwaving.

Crumb crusts take only a few minutes to prepare, and are microwaved just long enough to firm up.

Banana Cream Pie

1 9-in. microwaved crumb
    crust or pastry shell
1 small pkg. pudding mix
    (vanilla, chocolate,
    butterscotch), page 142
2 bananas

Makes 1 9-in. pie

Prepare pudding mix. Cool slightly. Slice 2 bananas into pie crust. Top with pudding. Cool. Garnish with whipped cream, if desired.

Graham Cracker Crust

5 tablespoons butter or
    margarine
1⅓ cups fine graham cracker
    crumbs
2 tablespoons white or
    brown sugar

Makes 9 or 10-in. crumb shell

Cookie Crumb Crust

Use finely crushed vanilla wafers, ginger snaps or chocolate wafers. Decrease butter to ¼ cup and omit sugar.

How to Microwave a Crumb Crust

Melt butter in a 9 or 10-in. pie plate at High, ¾ to 1 minute. Stir in crumbs and sugar until well moistened. Remove 2 tablespoons crumb mixture for garnish, if desired.

Press crumbs firmly and evenly against bottom and sides of plate. Microwave 1½ minutes, rotating ½ turn after 1 minute. Cool.

Microwave pastry shells before filling. Remove frozen pastry shells to glass pie plate. Before pricking, defrost 1½ to 2½ minutes at 50% power.

One Crust Pastry Shell

⅓ cup shortening
 1 to 2 tablespoons room temperature butter or margarine
 1 cup all purpose flour
½ teaspoon salt
 3 tablespoons cold water
 3 to 4 drops yellow food coloring

 Makes 9 or 10-in. pastry shell

Cut shortening and butter into flour and salt with a pastry blender until particles resemble coarse crumbs.

Combine water and food coloring. Sprinkle over pastry while stirring with fork, until dough is just moist enough to hold together.

Form into ball. Flatten to ½-in. Roll out on floured pastry cloth to scant ⅛-in. thick circle, 2-in. larger than inverted 9 or 10-in. pie plate.

Fit loosely into pie plate. Trim overhang to ½-in. Fold edge to form standing rim and flute.

How to Microwave a Pastry Shell

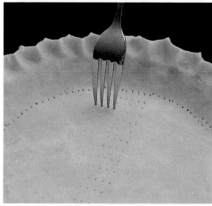

Prick crust with a fork at ⅛-in. intervals at bend of dish and ½-in. apart on bottom and sides of dish.

Microwave at High 6 to 7 minutes, rotating dish ½ turn after 3 minutes.

Check bottom of crust for doneness. It should be dry and opaque. A few brown spots may appear.

Lemon Pie

Serve lemon pie cool, topped with whipped cream.

1 9-in. microwaved crumb crust
   or pastry shell, page 132
1 cup sugar
4 tablespoons cornstarch

¼ teaspoon salt
1¾ cup water, divided
3 egg yolks, slightly beaten

2 tablespoons butter or
   margarine
1 tablespoon grated lemon peel
⅓ cup lemon juice

Makes 1 9-in. pie

Combine sugar, cornstarch, salt and ¼ cup water in a 1½-qt. casserole. Microwave remaining water at High 2 to 3 minutes until boiling.

Stir into sugar mixture. Microwave 4 to 6 minutes until very thick. Stir every 2 minutes. Mix a little hot mixture into egg yolks.

Blend yolks well into sugar mixture. Microwave 1 minute. Stir in butter, peel and juice. Cool slightly and turn into pie shell.

French Apple Pie

1 microwaved 9-in. pastry shell, with high fluted edge, page 132

Filling:
- 5 to 6 cups peeled, sliced apples
- 1 tablespoon lemon juice
- ½ cup sugar
- 2 tablespoons flour
- ½ teaspoon cinnamon or, ¼ teaspoon nutmeg

Topping:
- ¼ cup butter or margarine
- ½ cup flour
- ¼ cup brown or granulated sugar
- ½ teaspoon nutmeg

Makes 1 9-in. pie

How to Microwave French Apple Pie

Toss filling ingredients together. Pile high in pastry shell. Cut butter into other topping ingredients until crumbly. Sprinkle evenly over filling.

Place wax paper under plate while microwaving. Microwave at High 8 minutes. Rotate ½ turn. Microwave 6 to 10 minutes until apples are tender.

Fruit Pie

- 1 9-in. microwaved pastry or crumb crust, page 132
- 1 can (21-oz.) cherry or other pie filling

Makes 1 9-in. pie

Spread filling in pie shell. Microwave at High 7 to 10 minutes, rotating dish after 4 minutes until filling is hot and bubbly. Decorate with Pastry Cut Outs or reserved crumbs.

Pastry Cut Outs. Roll out leftover pastry to ⅛-in. thickness. Cut into 6 pieces with cookie cutter. Sprinkle with mixture of 1 teaspoon sugar and ⅛ teaspoon cinnamon. Arrange in ring on microwave baking sheet or wax paper. Microwave at High 2 to 4 minutes until dry and puffy, rotating after 2 minutes. Use to garnish fruit pies.

7-Minute One Dish Scratch Brownies

Fudgy or cake style brownies are America's favorite bar cookies. Mix and microwave a batch in about 7 minutes. Since corners receive more energy, shield them with foil to help brownies cook evenly. If you prefer not to shield, use a 9-inch round dish.

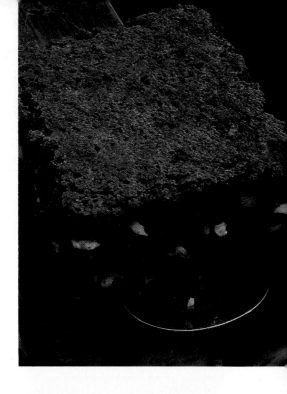

Fudgy Style

½ cup butter or margarine
6 tablespoons cocoa
1 cup sugar
1 egg
1 teaspoon vanilla
¾ cup all purpose flour
½ teaspoon baking powder
¼ teaspoon salt
½ cup chopped nuts

Cake Style

½ cup butter or margarine
6 tablespoons cocoa
¾ cup sugar
2 eggs
2 tablespoons milk
1 teaspoon vanilla
⅔ cup all purpose flour
½ teaspoon baking powder
¼ teaspoon salt
½ cup chopped nuts

Makes 12 to 16 brownies

How To Microwave Brownies

Place butter and cocoa in an 8-in. square dish. Microwave at High 1 to 1½ minutes, until butter melts.

Stir in sugar thoroughly. Adding the sugar first keeps cocoa mixture smooth and workable.

Add remaining ingredients in the order given and mix well.

Shield the top corners of the dish with foil triangles to prevent overcooking in the corners.

During microwaving, brownies puff up and puddles appear on top.

Microwave at High 5½ to 6 minutes, rotating ½ turn after 2, 4 and 5 minutes, until top is no longer wet.

Cool brownies directly on a heat-proof countertop. Trapped heat completes cooking on bottom of dish. Cool fudgy style for 30 minutes or cake style 10 to 15 minutes. Cut into squares; store tightly sealed.

Super S'mores

  2 graham cracker squares
  ⅓ (1.05-oz.) milk chocolate bar
  1 large marshmallow

Place 1 graham cracker square on a paper napkin to keep cracker crisp. Top with a chocolate piece and a marshmallow. Microwave at High just until marshmallow puffs, about 15 to 25 seconds. A marshmallow is high in sugar content and will scorch on the inside if overheated.

Multiple exposure, photographed through the oven door, reveals how marshmallow expands during microwaving. Watching through the oven door is the best way to judge timing.

Top with second ½ of cracker. Let S'more stand 1 minute so heat from marshmallow can melt chocolate.

Marshmallow Crispy Bars

¼ cup butter or margarine
5 cups miniature or 40 large
   marshmallows
¼ teaspoon salt
5 cups crispy rice cereal

Makes 36 squares

Variations:

**Marshmallow-Peanut
Crispies:** Thoroughly stir in 1
cup salted peanuts after cereal.

**Peanut Butter-Marshmallow
Crispies:** Add ¼ cup peanut
butter with marshmallows.

Chocolate-Peanut Crispies:
Add ¼ cup peanut butter and
½ cup chocolate chips with
marshmallows.

How to Microwave Marshmallow Crispy Bars

Melt butter in an 8×8-in. dish
at High power, 45 to 60 seconds. Stir in marshmallows
and salt.

Microwave 1½ to 2 minutes at
High until soft and melted,
stirring after 1 minute. Stir until
smooth before adding cereal.

Add cereal, ⅓ at a time, stirring with fork until well coated.
Press into dish with fork. Cool,
then cut into 1¼-in. squares.

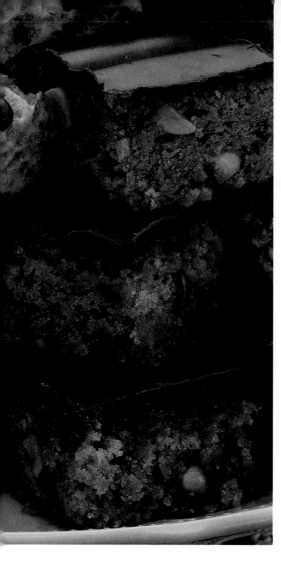

Peanut Scotch Bars

6 tablespoons butter or
   margarine
1 cup packed light brown
   sugar
¼ cup peanut butter
½ cup Spanish peanuts

2 eggs
1 cup all purpose flour
1 teaspoon vanilla
½ teaspoon baking powder
½ teaspoon salt

Makes 12 to 16 bars

How to Microwave Peanut Scotch Bars

Place butter in 8-in. square dish. Microwave at High until melted, 1 to 1½ minutes. Stir in sugar, peanut butter, then remaining ingredients. Spread evenly in dish. Shield corners (see Brownies, page 136).

Microwave at High 5½ to 7 minutes, rotating ¼ turn after 2, 4 and 5 minutes, until top is no longer wet. Cool as directed for brownies. Frost with Chocolate Chip Coating, page 149, using ½ cup chips.

Microwave Ideas with Store Bought Cookies

Select vanilla or chocolate wafers or shortbread cookies. Place on sheet of wax paper in oven. Times are the same for 1 to 6 cookies. Arrange in ring when doing several.

Marshmallow Toppers: Place ½ of a large marshmallow cut ▶ side down on cookie. Microwave at 50% power 15 to 30 seconds, just until marshmallow sticks to cookie. Frost with Chocolate Chip Coating, page 149.

Peanut-Mallow Sandwiches: Spread cookie with peanut butter. Top with 3 to 5 small marshmallows. Microwave at High 15 to 30 seconds, until marshmallows puff. Top with second cookie.

Mint Goodies: Place mint patty on cookie. Microwave at High 15 to 20 seconds, until patty is soft enough to stick to cookie. Cool.

Baked Apples

For each 2½ to 3-in. diameter apple:

1 tablespoon brown sugar
½ tablespoon butter

High Power
2 apples   2½-4½ min.
4 apples   4-6½ min.

Core apples. Place sugar and butter in cavities. Set in custard cups or arrange in ring in baking dish with space between. Cover tightly. Microwave, rotating after 2 minutes, until fork-tender. Let stand 2 minutes.

Apple Sauce

3 cups peeled, sliced apples
¼ cup water
½ cup sugar

Makes 2 to 2½ cups

Place fruit and water in 1½ to 2-qt. casserole. Cover. Microwave at High 5 to 9½ minutes, stirring after ½ the time, until fruit starts to turn transparent. Stir in sugar. Let stand, covered, 2 to 3 minutes. Stir before serving. Pureé, if desired.

Variations:

Pear Sauce: Substitute 3 cups peeled, sliced pears for apples.

Rhubarb Sauce: Substitute 2 cups 1-in. rhubarb pieces for apples.

Fruit Compote

1 cup sliced pears, peeled if desired
1 cup peeled, sliced peaches
1 cup cherries, pitted or whole
1 cup pineapple chunks
¼ cup water
¾ cup brown or granulated sugar

Makes approx. 1 quart

How to Microwave Fruit Compote

Combine fruit and water in a 1½ to 2-qt. casserole. Cover. Microwave at High 5½ to 8½ minutes, until fruit is almost tender, stirring after 4 minutes.

Stir in sugar. Re-cover fruit and let stand 2 minutes. Compotes may be served warm or cold.

140

Baked Pears

For each ½ of a firm 2½-in. diameter pear:

½ tablespoon brown sugar
½ tablespoon butter

High Power

4 halves	4-6½ min.
8 halves	7½-10½ min.

Halve and core pears. Arrange in baking dish with narrow ends toward center. Place sugar and butter in cavities. Cover. Microwave, rotating dish ½ turn after half the time. Let stand 2 minutes.

Apple Crisp

6 cups peeled, cored and
    sliced cooking apples
1 tablespoon lemon juice,
    optional

Topping:

 6 tablespoons butter
¾ cup packed brown sugar
¾ cup quick-cooking oats
½ cup flour
 1 teaspoon cinnamon

6 servings

Variation:

Cherry Crisp: Substitute 1 can
cherry pie filling for apples.
Microwave at High 8 to 11
minutes or until hot and bubbly
in center.

How to Microwave Apple Crisp

Place apples in 8-in. baking
dish. Sprinkle with lemon juice.
Melt butter in small mixing bowl
at High power 1 to 1½ minutes.

Stir in remaining ingredients
until crumbly. Sprinkle over
apples evenly; press down
lightly. Microwave at High 8
minutes. Rotate dish ½ turn.

Microwave 6 to 8 minutes until
apples are tender. Serve warm,
cold, plain or topped with
whipped cream or Lemon
Sauce, page 144.

How to Microwave a Pudding Mix

Place 1 package (3 to 3⅝-oz.)
pudding mix in 4-cup measure
or 1½-qt. casserole. Measure 2
cups milk; stir ⅓ cup into mix
until smooth; add remaining milk.

Microwave at High power 3
minutes. Stir. Microwave 1 to 4
minutes, stirring every minute,
until mixture boils.

Cool as directed on package
and pour into serving dishes
or pie shell. Mixture thickens
as it stands.

Baked Custard

1½ cups milk
¼ cup sugar
⅛ teaspoon salt
1 teaspoon vanilla
3 eggs, slightly beaten
Nutmeg or mace

4 servings

Variation:

Scald milk in 1-qt. casserole. Stir in egg mixture. Microwave at 50% power (Medium) 8 to 14 minutes, rotating ¼ turn every 3 minutes. Center will not be set, but will firm up while cooling.

How to Microwave Baked Custard

Pour milk into 2-cup measure or small bowl. Microwave at High 2 to 4 minutes, until hot but not boiling. Blend sugar, salt and vanilla into eggs lightly.

Stir mixture into milk. Pour into 4 6-oz. custard cups. Sprinkle with nutmeg or mace. Arrange in oven in ring. Microwave at 50% power 6 to 10 minutes.

Rotate and rearrange cups every 2 minutes until set. If custard starts to bubble or appears set, remove those that are baked.

Microwaved pudding mix makes a quick filling for pie.

Dessert Sauces

Dessert sauces are measured, mixed and microwaved in the same cup for easy preparation and clean-up. Sauces which need constant stirring conventionally are stirred once or twice during microwaving.

Hot Fudge Sauce

1 cup sugar
4 tablespoons cocoa
1 tablespoon flour
⅛ teaspoon salt
¾ cup milk

2 tablespoons butter or
   margarine
2 tablespoons light corn syrup
½ teaspoon vanilla

Makes about 1½ cups sauce

Combine dry ingredients in a 4-cup measure or 1½-qt. mixing bowl. Stir in milk. Add butter and syrup. Microwave at High 3 to 4 minutes until thick, smooth and a rich chocolate color. Stir in vanilla, mixing well. Serve hot or cold.

TIP: To reheat, microwave at High, covered with plastic wrap, 15 to 30 seconds for each ½ cup of sauce.

Tangy Lemon Sauce

½ cup sugar
1½ tablespoons cornstarch
⅛ teaspoon salt
1 cup water
2 tablespoons butter or
   margarine
2 to 3 tablespoons lemon
   juice
1 teaspoon grated lemon
   peel

Makes 1½ cups sauce

Combine sugar, cornstarch and salt in a 2 or 4-cup measure or mixing bowl. Stir in water; add butter. Microwave at High 4 to 6 minutes until thick and clear, stirring every 2 minutes. Stir in juice and peel. Serve warm or cold with Apple Crisp, page 142, gingerbread, steamed and bread puddings or over cake topped with whipped cream.

Butterscotch Sauce

1 cup packed brown sugar
¼ cup light corn syrup
1 tablespoon flour
2 tablespoons water
3 tablespoons butter or
    margarine
½ cup half & half

Makes 1½ cups sauce

Combine all ingredients in a 4-cup measure or 1½-qt. mixing bowl. Microwave at High 3 minutes. Stir. Microwave 4 to 6 minutes more until slightly thickened. Beat well. Serve warm over ice cream or other desserts.

Rum Butter Sauce

Serve Rum Butter Sauce over steamed puddings, gingerbread, pumpkin and spice cakes.

1 cup sugar
1 tablespoon cornstarch
¾ cup half & half
½ cup butter or margarine

2 tablespoons rum or 1
    teaspoon vanilla or rum
    extract
Dash nutmeg

Makes 2 cups sauce

How to Microwave Rum Butter Sauce

Combine sugar and cornstarch in a 1½-qt. casserole or 4-cup measure. Stir in cream; add butter. Microwave at High 3 minutes. Stir.

Microwave 3 to 4 minutes, until mixture has boiled hard for 2 minutes and is slightly thickened. Stir in flavorings until smooth.

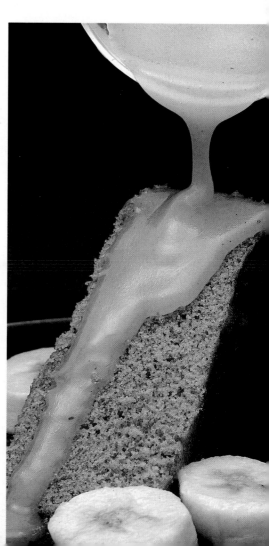

Candies

Old-fashioned candy making is a basic microwaving skill. Many conventional cooks feel that traditional candies are too difficult for beginners, but microwaving simplifies the cooking so much that flavorful old favorites are as easy to make as "short-cut" candies.

Do not use a conventional candy thermometer while microwaving. However, you may use the thermometer outside the oven to verify your cold water test, or to judge when candy is cool enough to work.

Old-Fashioned Fudge

2 cups sugar
5 tablespoons cocoa
¼ teaspoon salt
1 cup milk
1 tablespoon light corn syrup
3 tablespoons butter or
 margarine
1 teaspoon vanilla
½ cup chopped nuts, optional
Makes 1 pound

Penuche
Omit cocoa and substitute 1 cup brown sugar for 1 cup granulated sugar. Increase syrup to 2 tablespoons.

How to Microwave Old-Fashioned Fudge

Combine sugar, cocoa and salt in a 3 to 3½-qt. mixing bowl or casserole. Stir in milk and syrup thoroughly. Add butter.

Cover. Microwave at High 5 minutes. Mix well. Microwave uncovered 10 to 14 minutes.

Test by dropping a small amount of mixture in ice water. It should form a soft ball when picked up.

Cool mixture, without stirring, to lukewarm (120° on edges). After 10 minutes casserole may be placed in bowl of cool water, if desired.

Add vanilla and nuts; beat until mixture is thick and creamy, starts to lose its shine and hold its shape.

Pour quickly into buttered plate or 9×5 or 10×6-in. loaf dish. If fudge is too thick to spread, stir in a few drops cream or milk.

Quick Chocolate Candies

Chocolate melts smoothly in the microwave oven without danger of scorching. With Chocolate Chip Coating you can make a variety of quick and simple candies. Use it to dip large nuts, marshmallows, pretzels, animal crackers or other small cookies. Use 2 forks for easy dipping. The large recipe can also frost a 13×9-in. pan of bars or 5 to 6 dozen cookies. If coating sets up while dipping, microwave 10 to 20 seconds to remelt. Refrigerate candies for faster setting.

Turtlettes

4 dozen large pecans, halved
    lengthwise
2 dozen large pecans, halved
    crosswise
2 dozen caramel candies
1 small recipe Chocolate Chip
    Coating, opposite

Makes 2 dozen

How to Microwave Turtlettes

Arrange pecans on a sheet of wax paper with 4 long halves for legs and 1 short half for head of each Turtlette. Do 6 Turtlettes at a time.

Butter a pie plate well. Arrange 6 caramels evenly around edge. Microwave at High 15 to 30 seconds, until soft but not melted on bottom. Cover with wax paper to keep warm.

Press caramel down firmly over nuts. Quickly, form into turtle shape with fingers. If caramels become hard, microwave 5 to 10 seconds.

Peanut Butter Haystacks

1 cup (6-oz.) butterscotch
  chips
½ cup peanut butter

½ cup salted peanuts
2 cups chow mein noodles

Makes about 2½ dozen

How to Microwave Peanut Butter Haystacks

Place chips and peanut butter in 2-qt. casserole or bowl. Cover with plastic wrap.

Microwave at 50% power (Medium) 3 to 5 minutes, until most of chips are shiny or soft.

Blend well. Stir in peanuts and chow mein noodles with rubber spatula.

Drop by forkfuls onto wax paper. Cool until set.

How to Microwave Chocolate Chip Coating

Frost with Chocolate Chip Coating. Or, using 2 forks, dip Turtlette in chocolate. Place on wax paper. Cool until set.

Place 1 cup chips and 2 table-spoons vegetable shortening (not butter) or ½ cup chips and 1 tablespoon shortening in bowl. Cover with plastic wrap.

Microwave at 50% power (Medium) 2½ to 4 minutes until most of the chips are shiny and soft. Stir well. Use to frost cookies or dip candies.

10-Minute Peanut Brittle

1 cup sugar
½ cup light corn syrup
⅛ teaspoon salt
1 to 1½ cups roasted, salted peanuts

1 tablespoon butter or margarine
1 teaspoon vanilla
1 teaspoon soda

Makes 1 pound

Very-Thin Peanut Brittle
Cool mixture on cookie sheet 3 to 5 minutes. Lift from sheet and pull or stretch mixture to desired thinness.

How to Microwave Peanut Brittle

Combine sugar, syrup and salt in 2-qt. casserole or mixing bowl. Microwave at High 5 minutes.

Stir in peanuts. Microwave 2 to 5 minutes, stirring after 2 and 4 minutes, until syrup and peanuts are lightly browned.

Stir in butter, vanilla and soda until light and foamy. Spread to ¼-in. thickness on large, well-buttered cookie sheet.

Bark Candy

1 pound confectioners' or candy coating (vanilla, chocolate, butterscotch or caramel)
1 cup of any of the following: roasted, salted nuts (unblanched almonds, peanuts, walnuts, pecans or mixed nuts) sunflower seeds or soya nuts, raisins

Makes approx. 1¼ pounds

If candy coating is in a solid piece, break into squares. Place in a single layer in a 2-qt. casserole. Microwave at 50% power (Medium) 3 to 5 minutes, until pieces are soft, stirring after 3 minutes.

Add nuts, seeds or raisins. Stir until candy coating is smooth and completely melted.

Spread on wax paper to ¼-in. thickness. Cool until hard, then break into pieces.

150

Convenience Foods

Many convenience foods now include microwave instructions on the packages. Most of them can be microwaved to serving temperature in far less time than it takes conventionally. Even foods which you finish in a conventional oven become more convenient when you microwave-defrost them first.

How to Microwave TV Dinners   High Power, 7½-11 min.

Remove foil-lined lid from tray. Place dessert in custard cup and set aside. Remove any bread.

Cover tray with wax paper and place in oven. Microwave at High for ½ the total time.

Turn main course over; stir vegetables. Microwave remaining time. Microwave dessert 20 to 30 seconds, or cook in toaster oven.

How to Microwave Family-Size Entreés   High Power, 8-10 min. per lb.

Preheat browning grill 5 minutes at High. Loosen lid from foil pan. If lid is foil-lined, replace it with wax paper cut to same size.

Place pan on grill. Be sure wax paper does not touch grill. Microwave at High, rotating pan ½ turn after ½ the cooking time.

Heat from grill defrosts bottom of food, making it unnecessary to remove from foil pan. After heating let stand, covered, 5 minutes or as package directs.

How to Defrost Orange Juice or Lemonade

Remove one metal lid from 6-oz. can of frozen orange juice. Place upright in oven. Microwave at High ½ to 1½ minutes.

Concentrate should be softened but not warm. Pour into container and stir in cold water as directed on package.

How to Microwave Fully-Cooked Fried Chicken   High Power, 1 lb., 9-11 min.; 2 lb., 15-17 min.

Separate chicken pieces and arrange on roasting rack in single layer with meatiest portions to outside of dish.

Cover with paper towel. Microwave at High for ½ the time. Rearrange pieces, but do not turn over. Cover.

Microwave remaining time. Remove to plate lined with paper towels. Cover with paper towel and let stand 2 to 3 minutes to crisp.

How to Defrost Frozen Bread Dough

Measure 1 to 1½ cups water into a 12×8-in. baking dish. Microwave at High until boiling. Heavily grease an 8×4 or 9×5-in. loaf dish. Butter frozen dough on all sides.

Place in loaf dish set in hot water. Cover with wax paper. Microwave at 50% power (Medium) 2 minutes, rotating ¼ turn every minute. Turn dough over.

Microwave and rotate 2 minutes more. Let stand 10 minutes. Dough should be defrosted and slightly warm. If not, microwave and rotate, 1 minute at a time, until ready.

153

How to Defrost Frozen 2-Crust Pies and Pot Pies   50% Power (Medium), 5½-9 min. per lb.

Remove pie from metal pan to a suitable glass pie plate, inverted 1½-qt. casserole lid or an individual casserole.

Microwave at 50% power (Medium), rotating after ½ the time. Pie is defrosted when a wooden pick can be inserted in center.

Bake conventionally as directed on package for ½ to ⅔ suggested time. Do not defrost 1-crust custard pies before baking.

How to Defrost Cakes and Brownies   30% Power (Low), 1½-3½ min. per lb.

Remove cake or brownies from foil pan. Place on plate lined with paper towel.

Microwave at 30% power (Low), rotating after ½ the time. Lower power level is necessary or frosting will melt. Watch whipped cream frosting carefully.

Test by inserting a wooden pick into center of cake or brownies. Pick should meet little or no resistance.

How to Defrost Cream Pies   30% Power (Low), ¾-2 min. per lb.

Remove pie from foil pan to plate or pie dish. Microwave at 30% Power (Low).

Test by inserting wooden pick in center of pie. It should meet no resistance. Let stand 5 minutes, if needed, to complete defrosting.

Index